OUR
INCOMPARABLE
GOD

To my "Indian" Sister

In Christs' Grace

Barry L. Ross

OUR
INCOMPARABLE
GOD

A COMMENTARY ON ISAIAH 40-55

BARRY L. ROSS

FOUNTAIN PRESS
PUNE

Our Incomparable God
A Commentary on Isaiah 40–55

Barry L. Ross

ISBN: 81-88784-00-1

Fountain Press, PB No. 1455, Pune, 411037, India
www.fountainpress.org

CONTENTS

PREFACE

In 1994, while guest lecturing at Union Biblical Seminary, Pune, India, I was assigned to teach a course on the Old Testament Prophets, with a focus on Isaiah 40-55. I began to write sections of "commentary" on the Isaiah chapters for my students, continuing over the next two years. During that time, I was based in Japan as a missionary, and was writing for two denominational monthly papers. One of these papers, the *Immanuel Kyoho,* serialized my "commentary" in Japanese translation over a two-year period. The English version, in photocopy manuscript format, has continued to be used at Union Biblical Seminary as a resource for the students in the Prophets course. The present book is a revised publication of this earlier work. Much thanks goes to Dr. Paulson Pulikottil, my Old Testament teaching colleague at Union Biblical Seminary, and his wife Sheila for their skills in editing this book and bringing it to publication. Their suggestions for content and structure have been invaluable. I dedicate this book to Margaret, my wife of 43 years, who encouraged me during the earlier writing and teaching of the Prophets course, and during the process of bringing this book to publication. This is dedicated also to my numerous former students in some ten Asian countries and North America where I have taught and lectured during my 35 years of classroom teaching.

INTRODUCTION

Isaiah of Jerusalem lived and preached in the late eighth and early seventh centuries B.C., perhaps about 760—695 B.C. However, the collection of his prophecies, as contained in the canonical book of Isaiah, speak to *three historical periods* in Israel's life.

Chapters 1–39 are historically within Isaiah's own lifetime, from about 739—701 B.C. In this period *Assyria* was dominant. The Assyrian armies invaded and occupied Israel, the northern Jewish Kingdom in 722 B.C., largely deporting the ten northern tribes into a widely scattered Assyrian exile. In 701 B.C., the Assyrian armies invaded and briefly occupied the southern Jewish Kingdom of Judah, but its capital Jerusalem escaped capture. The Assyrian army withdrew and life in Judah went on "as usual."

Chapters 40–55 are set prophetically within the years 605—539 B.C. In this period *Babylon* was dominant. These years include the periods of Judah's exile in Babylon, beginning with Babylon's first invasion of Judah in 605 B.C., including Jerusalem's destruction in 587 B.C., and concluding just before the demise of the Babylonian Empire in 539 B.C.

Chapters 56–66 are set prophetically within the years *539—500 B.C.* (or perhaps 400 B.C.). In this period *Persia* was dominant. In 539 B.C., the Persian King Cyrus brought about the downfall of the Babylonian Empire with his conquest of

Introduction

Babylon. In 538 B.C., he decreed that all exiled peoples throughout the former Assyrian and Babylonian Empires may return to their original homelands. This included the Jews. Thus, the years 539 B.C. and beyond encompass the various returns of the Jews to Jerusalem and Judea.

Long before Judah would go into exile, Isaiah preached and wrote his message of hope and deliverance. He foresaw that in a future day the Jews in Babylonian captivity would believe that God had abandoned them (Isa 40:27). Thus, they would desperately need his message.

Surrounded by pagan gods who *seemed* to have given Babylon her great power, these despairing Jews needed to know once again that it was *Yahweh*, the God who had overpowered the so-called gods of Egypt in a time long before, who would now show himself to be greater that Babylon's gods, Bel and Nebo. And the demonstration of his power would again be as in the past—he would lead his people out from Babylon and into the land of Judah, just as he had from Egypt to Canaan long before. A despairing, dejected people without hope, they needed to know that *Yahweh, the living Creator, is incomparable and sovereign.* All nations, all rulers, all so-called gods, indeed all elements of creation were subject to him and to no other.

They needed to know that in contrast to the transitory nature of "the people" (i.e., Babylon), "the word of our God stands forever" (Isa 40:7–8).

They needed to know that because their God, the Lord, "neither faints nor is weary," they, too, would again "run and not be weary . . . walk and not faint" (Isa 40:28, 31).

They needed to know that their God, the Lord, "the first and with the last" (Isa 41:4), is always contemporary with history. The Lord is never out of date!

10

They needed to know that though nations and rulers rise and strut about this earth, they are but actors on God's stage, and when the curtain falls upon scene after scene,

> All the nations are as nothing before Him,
> They are regarded by Him as less than nothing and meaningless (Isa 40:17).

> He it is who reduces rulers to nothing,
> Who makes the judges of the earth meaningless (Isa 40:23).

And their gods?

> Behold, all of them are false,
> Their works are worthless,
> Their molten images are wind and emptiness (Isa 41:29).

They needed to know that once again barren Jerusalem and Judah would so overflow with children that God would command:

> Enlarge the place of your tent;
> Stretch out the curtains of your dwellings, spare not;
> Lengthen your cords,
> And strengthen your pegs (Isa 54:2–3).

They needed to hear the ringing invitation: "Ho! Everyone who thirsts, come to the waters" (Isa 55:1).

> And let him return to the Lord,
> And He will have compassion on him;
> And to our God,
> And He will abundantly pardon (Isa 55:7).

They needed to hear the heart-stirring assurance:

> You will go out [from Babylon] with joy,
> And be led forth with peace;
> The mountains and the hills will break forth into shouts of joy before you,

11

Introduction

> And all the trees of the field will clap their hands [as you . . .
> pass by on your triumphant march to Jerusalem!]
> (Isa 55:12).

And *we*, today, in the twenty-first century A.D., need to hear this same message. We need to know that the God who brought Israel out of exile is still the same One who brings us from the darkness of sin into the light of His glorious salvation.

We, too, need to hear afresh the call to return unto our God, and in that returning become the witness that our God is incomparable, and hear God say of us: *[This is] the people whom I formed for Myself* (Isa 43:21a), and discover anew that we are chosen by God to be His people for only one purpose, the same purpose for which He chose Israel: *[To] declare My praise* (Isa 43:21b).

To declare God's praise is the reason for our existing as the People of God. Peter, in the New Testament, about A.D. 63 or 64 reaffirmed this when he wrote to Christians in northern Asia Minor (modern-day Turkey) who were facing persecution from non-Christians and government officials: "You are a chosen race, a royal priesthood, a holy nation, a people for God's own possession, that you may proclaim the excellencies of Him who has called you out of darkness into His marvelous light; for you once were not a people, but now you are the people of God; you had not received mercy, but now you have received mercy." (1 Pet 2:9–10).

COMFORT, O COMFORT MY PEOPLE!
(ISAIAH 40)

There are three major units in chapter 40:

❑ Prelude: God is Coming (vv. 1–11)
❑ The Uniqueness of the Lord (vv. 12–26)
❑ The Foolishness of Unbelief (vv. 27–31)

40:1–11. Good News! God is Coming

Verses (40:) 1–2 set the *fundamental theme* for this entire segment of Isaiah's prophecy (chapters 40–55): *encouragement and comfort.* The command, "Comfort, O comfort My people!" in the Hebrew is plural, not addressed to one person, but to many. But addressed to whom? Prophets in general? It is not clear. The emphasis here is not on "who," but on the abundance of comfort that is to be made available. Even the Hebrew words are beautiful in sound: *naḥamu, naḥamu.* Here is to be the reversal of the abject despair reflected in the words of the later (seventh—sixth century) prophet Jeremiah concerning fallen "widow" Jerusalem: "She has none to comfort her" (Lam 1:2. See also 1:9, 16, 21). It is *God* who will give the comfort. In the Hebrew verbal form that is used here, comfort is "to give active help." God's active intervention is on the way! The psalmist David spoke of God's active intervention in a certain despairing circumstance of his life: "You, LORD have helped me and comforted me" (Ps 86:17).

When promising this comfort, the Lord speaks in covenant language: "My people . . . your God." Such words look back, reminding the people that at the first Exodus, when establishing His covenant with Israel, God had said, "I will take you for My people, and I will be your God" (Exod 6:7). Now, to Israel in exile, will come the fulfillment of Hosea's prophecy: "Then I will say to those who were not My people, 'You are My people!' And they will say, 'You are my God!'" (Hos 2:23).[1]

These words provide a link with God's promise through the prophet Jeremiah, spoken when the destruction of Jerusalem was imminent, looking forward to a restored and forgiven Israel:

> "The days are coming," says the Lord, "when I will make a new covenant with the house of Israel and . . . Judah . . . and I will be their God and they will be my people" (Jer 31:31; see also 24:7; 30:22; 32:38).

The command to comfort God's people is reinforced with the words, "Speak tenderly," literally, "speak to the heart." This is language of intimacy, kindness and love. The patriarch Joseph, wronged by his brothers, "comforted [*naham*] and spoke to their hearts" (Gen 50:21). Ruth responded to Boaz's words of approval and praise with, "You have comforted [*naham*] me and have spoken to the heart of your maidservant" (Ruth 2:13).

Here in Isaiah, "Jerusalem" is the recipient of God's comfort, yet the prophecy is addressed to the exiles in Babylon.

---

[1] For other instances of the use of "My people" see Exodus 19:5; Deuteronomy 4:20; 7:6; 2 Samuel 7:24, and of "Your God" see Genesis 17:7; Exodus 29:45, 46; Leviticus 26:12, 13, 45; Deuteronomy 29:13; Revelation 21:7.

Jerusalem, however, is personified and paralleled with "My people," thus signifying, not just the physical place, but also the community of God's people.[2]

The content of the comfort spoken to the heart of God's people is that "her warfare has ended [and] her iniquity has been removed." Such gracious words! For generations God's people had known the ravages of war—from her small neighbors, Syria, Ammon, Moab, Philistia, and from the great powers, Egypt, Assyria and Babylon. Much of this was "from the Lord's hand double for all her sins." But now the word of comfort is "O, My people, you have suffered more than enough for your sins. You have paid the just penalty. My word of long ago has been fulfilled: 'If you do not obey Me, then I will punish you seven times more for your sins' (Lev 26:18). But now it is time for blessing, pardon and restoration." Such a word of comfort, such giving of active help is accompanied by pardon and forgiveness in instances mentioned above: Joseph's brothers ask, "Please forgive [our] transgression" (Gen 51:17); David declares, "You, Lord, are good, and ready to forgive, and abundant in lovingkindness . . . a God merciful and gracious" (Ps 86:5, 15).

Verses (40:) 3–5 focus on "a highway for our God" (v. 3). Isaiah overhears a voice commanding that preparations be made for the arrival of the Lord, for He is returning to Jerusalem. This highway is for both God and His people to travel as they go up together from Babylon to Jerusalem. Here is a link back to Isaiah 11:16: "There will be a highway for the remnant of His people . . . as it was for Israel in the day that he

---

[2] For New Testament personifications of Jerusalem, see Galatians 4:26; Hebrews 12:22–23; Revelation 21:2, 10.

came up from the land of Egypt" (NKJV) (though the context of Isaiah 11 is of the Messianic kingdom; thus the "highway" here refers to some return connected with the setting up of Christ's kingdom). Both these references are reminiscent of the first Exodus, and in so doing present *the theme of a new Exodus.* And for this new Exodus, every obstacle to God's progress must be removed: metaphorically, leveling the ground, straightening the road, and building a raised highway. In historical reality there were, in fact, many obstacles to what God was about to do for His people, the main one being the rule of Babylon which must be overthrown, and the changing of the exiled Jews' unbelief to renewed belief in the abilities of the Lord, God the Creator.

And in the new Exodus, "the glory of the Lord" is to be revealed. In the context here this is intended to bring to mind the glory of God's great acts of redemption in Israel's past history, especially the signs and wonders connected with the first Exodus. Numbers 14:21–22 speaks of "all the earth [being] filled with the glory of the Lord" because of "My glory and My signs which I did in Egypt and in the wilderness." Ezekiel, prophesying in the early part of the Exile, in a vision saw "the glory of the Lord" leave Jerusalem (Ezek 11:23). But he also saw a future vision of the glory returning to fill the Temple (Ezek 43:1–5).

While Ezekiel's vision localizes the "glory" to Jerusalem and the Temple, Isaiah universalizes it: "all flesh," all mankind shall see God's glory "together," that is, simultaneously and suddenly. But what is the "glory" of the Lord? Here in Isaiah it is the salvation that God will render on behalf of His people, their deliverance from their Babylonian enslavement. The good word is that salvation is not for them alone, but is to be extended to the whole of mankind. Here is a link with some of

16

the songs of the Psalm writers, such as Psalm 96, which sings: "Say among the nations, 'The Lord reigns'" (v. 10); "Proclaim good tidings of His salvation from day to day" (v. 2); and "Tell of His glory among the nations, His wonderful deeds among all the peoples" (vv. 2–3).

This is still the purpose of God's saving act of grace today. *We,* God's redeemed ones, are God's glory, that others may look upon us and say, "Who is like you, a people saved by the Lord?" (Deut 33:29).

Verses (40:) 6–8 contrast the *transience of humankind* and the *permanence of God's word* (vv. 7–8). Again Isaiah hears "a voice," the same as in verse 3 when this voice was "calling out." Now the command is for the *prophet* to "call out" (v. 6). The message is one of hope and encouragement to the Jewish captives.

The content of the message draws on a metaphor from nature. "Flesh," that is, humankind, and "grass" arc compared. They arc the same. Humankind has a "loveliness" or beauty like the flowering grass of the field. "Loveliness" here in the Hebrew is *ḥesed,* essentially meaning "faithfulness" or "durability."[3]

So here, today, is the beautiful flower, giving pleasure to the eye, but when I look tomorrow it is no more, dried and withered by the wind. Even so is the durability of mankind. It is as fickle as the flowers. But why is this *good* news to the discouraged Jewish captives? Surely they need no reminder of their weakness and shortness of lifespan. This "good" news is *to* the Jews but not *about* them, for while "all flesh" is indeed like the grass, it is specifically "the people," here signifying *Babylon* upon whom the "breath of the Lord" will blow. This is Babylon

---

[3] NIV translates it as "glory" whereas NRSV has "constancy."

the powerful, the same Babylon who, in an earlier prophecy Isaiah says, "used to strike *the peoples*" (the Jews and other ethnic groups, Isa 14:6), the same Babylon who,

> Made the earth tremble,
> Who shook kingdoms,
> Who made the earth like a wilderness
> And overthrew its cities (Isa 14:16–17).

Now, God will turn history upside-down. When the "breath [or "wind," Heb. *ruah*] of the Lord" blows upon "the people" He will

> Cut off from Babylon name and survivors,
> Offspring and posterity . . .
> [Babylon will be made] a possession for the hedgehog,
> And swamps of water (Isa 14:22–23).

Judah's captor, who it seemed to them would never fall, whose durability seemed assured forever, is but a flowering field grass, here this morning, gone tonight. The reality of the non-durability, the transience of Babylon, will reveal the utter unreality and hollowness of the earlier Nebuchadnezzar's boast:

> I will raise my throne above the stars of God . . .
> I will make myself like the Most High (Isa 14:13–14).

But the question remains: If an empire like Babylon cannot endure, if all kingdoms wither at the mere breath of God, is there anything that does endure? Is there anything to give God's people hope? Amidst the shifting sands of international politics and destruction is there something to grasp hold of? The answer is, yes, yes indeed! It is the "word of our God," a word that "stands forever" (Isa 40:8).

In the present context, Isaiah does not mean simply "these words I am now speaking, this particular prophecy." Rather, he means *the* Word (singular in the Hebrew) of God, that is, the active will and declared purpose of God. This is what is permanent. This declaration of the permanency of God's Word serves to mark the opening and closing of Isaiah's prophecy of hope to the Jewish Exiles, for it is taken up again when the Lord says,

> So shall My word be which goes forth from My mouth;
> It shall not return to Me empty,
> Without accomplishing what I desire,
> And without succeeding in the matter for which I sent it
>   (Isa 55:11).

Thus, at both the beginning and the ending of the prophecy there is the assurance and reassurance to the exiles that what God says He will do, He will indeed do it. The Exiles indeed *"will* go out with joy, and be led forth with peace" (Isa 55:12).

Verses (40:) 9–11 speak of a *messenger* bearing the *good news of the Shepherd-God.* Jerusalem is the messenger. She has heard the news; she must pass it on to the towns of Judah. And the message is: "Look, God is coming to Jerusalem/Judah!"

The emphasis is upon the *power* of God, that is, His *redeeming* strength. Isaiah uses the terms "might" and "arm." Here we hear echoes of Moses' long ago stirring sermon to the Israelites after the first Exodus: "[Has any other] god tried to take for himself a nation from within another nation by . . . a mighty hand and by an outstretched arm . . . as the Lord your God did for you in Egypt?" (Deut 4:34), or even Moses' earlier reminder to God, Himself, when God wanted to destroy the Israelites, that these are "Your people whom You have brought out from the land of Egypt with great power and with a mighty hand" (Exod 32:11).

And when God arrives at Jerusalem He will bring his "reward" (v. 10) with Him. This reward is composed of the Jewish prisoners, the exiles newly released from Babylon. Again we hear echoes of the Exodus (compare Isa 62:11; Rev 22:12).

19

Then, in verse 11, Isaiah makes an abrupt shift, with emphasis now upon the *tenderness* of the Shepherd-God. He "tends His flock," He "gathers the lambs" and "carries them in His bosom," He "gently leads the nursing [mother sheep]."

"Shepherd" is a political term for Israel's kings. Thus the compassionate quality of the Lord's leadership is stressed. Here we see Isaiah anticipating the shepherdship of God as later pictured by Ezekiel:

> I [the Lord], Myself will search for my sheep and seek them out. As a shepherd cares for his herd . . . so I will care for My sheep and will deliver them from all the places to which they were scattered . . . I will feed My flock and I will lead them to rest . . . I will seek the lost, bring back the scattered, bind up the broken, and strengthen the sick (Ezek 34:11–12, 15–16).

This, too, is reminiscent of the former Exodus, though Moses uses a different metaphor when he reminds the Israelites just before crossing into Canaan: "In the wilderness . . . you saw how the Lord your God carried you, just as a man carries his son, in all the way which you have walked" (Deut 1:31).

How different will be God's shepherdship when seen in opposition to the exploitative leadership of the past kings, the "shepherds of Israel" of whom God says:

> Those who were sickly you have not strengthened, the diseased you have not healed, the broken you have not bound up, the scattered you have not brought back, nor have you sought the lost; but with force and with severity you have dominated them (Ezek 34:1, 4).[4]

---

[4] For other passages where shepherd language in applied to the Lord, compare Psalm 23; Luke 15:3–7; John 10:1–18.

40:12–26. The Uniqueness of the Lord

Verses 40:1–11 (studied above) is a prelude that has set the theme of the whole prophecy in chapters 40–55. This theme is one of comfort and promise to the Jewish exiles in Babylon: "God is about to do something marvelous! Get ready to march!"

But in the historical context to which Isaiah addressed this message there was a very real obstacle to accepting this message. This obstacle is summed up in verse 27, a key verse to understanding what Isaiah is doing in this chapter. The depressed exiles, God's people, have a wrong understanding of God: "God is not dealing fairly with us," they complain. Thus, there is the *obstacle of complaint and unbelief.* So, in order to remove this obstacle, Isaiah launches into a marvelous description of the uniqueness, power and strength of the Lord in verses 12–26. The corrective to the exiles' complaining and unbelief is a *revival of the praises of the Lord.*

Verses (40:) 12–17 describe the *immeasurability of the Lord.* Isaiah puts forth a rhetorical question: "Who has measured . . .?" (v. 12). The sense of the question is somewhat ambiguous. On the one hand, Isaiah is asking, "Can anyone measure . . .?" with the expected reply, "Of course not!" On the other hand, he is asking, "Who actually has measured . . .?" with the expected reply, "Only God Himself."

Isaiah lists the three basic forms of measurement: *quantity, area, weight.* He mentions the largest observable things of nature we can see: the oceans, "the waters in the hollow of His hand," (The Dead Sea Scroll Isaiah manuscript reads "the waters of the sea"); the sky, the soil, the mountains and hills.[5] To us, such things are quite immeasurable, even though they are finite and theoretically *could* be measured. For instance, how impossible it seems to "mark off the heavens by the span" (NASB), that is, using a ridiculously short measure of only a half-cubit (about 23 centimeters or 7/8 inch), or how impossible to find a balance scale large enough to weigh even one small hill, to say nothing of a large mountain. The implied response to the impossible is that it *is* possible, for God can, and has, measured the immeasurable, weighed the unweighable, leaving a further implied question: *how immeasurable must God Himself be?*

Lest the exiles (and we today) think Isaiah is referring to some abstract force or universal power, he makes it clear that he is talking about a living, thinking, planning *Person.* Again he puts forth a series of rhetorical questions (vv. 13–14): "Who has directed [or measured] the Spirit of the Lord . . . informed Him . . . given Him understanding . . . taught him . . . justice and . . . knowledge?" The implication of these questions is that, just as we have no measure capable of measuring created things (v. 12), how much less have we any standard by which to make judgments or any right to inform God about something or advise Him on what He does, says or decides. Here we are reminded of the rhetorical questions the Lord, in another setting, threw at Job: "Who set its [the earth's] measurements? Who enclosed the sea with doors?" (Job 38:5, 8), and more, in delayed response to Job's earlier complaint that "God has

---

[5] The text of our Bibles today is based mainly on what we call the Hebrew Massoretic Text (MT), dating from about the tenth century A.D. The Dead Sea Scrolls (DSS) date from about the first century B.C., 1,000 years earlier.

wronged me . . . He has . . . considered me as His enemy."
(Job 19: 6, 10). And Job *does* grasp a new, larger vision of God
and repents of his uninformed complaining: "I have declared
that which I did not understand, things . . . which I did not
know . . . But now my eye sees You" (Job 42:3, 5). Job's *spiritual
eyes* were opened and he now sees that God is still *for* him. The
unnamed composer of Psalm 118 likewise declares, "[when] all
nations surrounded me" (v. 10), "from my distress I called upon
the Lord" (v. 5), and he learned that "the Lord is *for* me" (v.6).

An important principle is illustrated here (in Isaiah, in Job
and in Psalm 118): we need right thinking about God before we
can grasp and apply His promises. A narrow concept of God
will get in the way of full experience of His power and promise.

Isaiah now moves from the world of nature to the world of
humankind and history (vv. 15–17). He points out that since the
Lord is Himself so immeasurable, even "the nations" are totally
insignificant in comparison to Him. Isaiah continues the
measuring metaphor. How small in volume is one "drop from a
bucket." How weightless is one "speck of dust on the scales."
"All the nations" together are but a drop and a speck. They
"weigh" nothing. Isaiah is not being contemptuous of the
nations. They do, indeed, have their usefulness in God's plan
for humankind. Rather, he simply is saying that in God's sight
their claims and pretensions have no weight. In fact, they are
"less than nothing and meaningless [or "void"]." The Hebrew
here is *tohu*, the same term used in Genesis 1:1 to describe the
condition of the universe before God brought order into it.
Thus, just as the universe was useless, serving no purpose in
God's design for history without His active presence, so the
nations have no value apart from God's active presence. They
are "nothing" in themselves!

This was a very important truth to put into the hearts of the Jewish exiles, since they were in exile in the midst of the most powerful nation and empire of that day—Babylon. In that context, verses 15 and 17 are remarkable assertions.

Verses (40:) 18–24 highlight the *incomparability of the Lord*. Again Isaiah poses a rhetorical question, "To whom then will you liken God?" but the expected *negative* answer is very important: there is no "likeness" possible for God. He cannot be compared with anything. This is related to the First and Second commandments (Exod 20:3–4). The Lord, as the one true living God, is unique. Thus, it is futile to make images of Him.

This thought leads Isaiah to a brief, contemptuous digression on the absurdity of idolatry (vv. 19–20). "An idol!" is posed as a possible answer to the question of verse 18. The prophet scorns such a suggestion. Whether the idol of a rich man (v. 19) or the idol of a poor man (v. 20), such things are to be pitied. (This theme is taken up more fully in chapter 41.)

In verses 21–24 Isaiah returns to his main theme. He now gives substance to his claim of God's greatness by reminding the exiles of their great national memories and traditions: "Have you not known? Have you not heard?" He extols God as Creator (v. 22). He extols God's kingship over all the kings of men. The "rulers" and "judges," like the nations themselves, are subject to God's sovereign rule over history. This was another important truth for captive Israel (and us!) to be reminded of.

Verses (40:) 25–26 declare the *cosmic sovereignty of the Lord*. Earlier, in verse 18, Isaiah had asked, "To whom will you liken God?" Now, the Lord Himself interrupts Isaiah, speaking in the first person to the exiles, as if to say, "Are you listening to what my prophet is saying? Is there anyone or anything like me?" (v. 25).

Our Incomparable God

Then Isaiah resumes, with the climax to the whole series of comparisons so far (v. 26): "Look up!" as if to ask, "What do you see?" And the answer, of course, is *the stars*. But Isaiah is too contemptuous even to call them by their name. Rather, "see who has created *these*." This was a very powerful question in the historical circumstances, for the stars were the main deities of Babylon. They were thought to be very powerful in their control of human affairs, giving impetus to the highly developed Babylonian religio-science of astrology (still very much alive in secular man's thinking today!). For the Jewish exiles, the stars must have come to represent the very strength of Babylon, their conquerors. Indeed, we know that many of the Jews, themselves, had already begun honoring the stars as deities while yet in Judah, even before the destruction of Jerusalem (see Jer 8:2, "host of heaven"). So the question and its answer are significant in the circumstances.

Isaiah asks a double question: Who *created* the stars? Who *controls* the stars? As to the first, Isaiah uses the Hebrew verb *bara*, used only with God as its subject, a special word for creation (used, for instance, in Gen 1:1). The answer to this first question, then, implies that the stars are only created *things*—not gods—and merely part of the universe that God has measured and weighed!

As to who controls these created stars, Isaiah uses a very bold metaphor. He pictures the stars as an army under God's direct command! There is humor here. They are not even "officers." They are nothing but "privates" in God's army. They must even "number off" and answer to His orders.

Thus, from verses 12–26, as a corrective to the exiles' wrong thinking about God, Isaiah has painted on his canvas a marvelous view of God's immeasurable, incomparable, cosmic sovereignty over nature, history, humanity, rulers, and over everything that men turn into gods for themselves. But this view was not intended only for the Jewish exiles of some 2,500 years ago. It is the view of God meant for God's people in all times, in all places. This same view, if spread before *our* spiritual eyes, if painted on *our* hearts, will place all things around us into proper perspective.

40.27–31. The Foolishness of Unbelief

Verse (40:) 27 is the key to understanding what Isaiah is teaching in this chapter. Again he throws a question at the exiles, but this time not rhetorical. The Hebrew says: "Why do you keep on saying, *O Jacob,* and keep on speaking, *O Israel* ?"[6] And what they are continually saying is a *complaint* : "*My way* (Heb., *derek*) is hidden from *the Lord,* and *my justice* (Heb., *mishpat*) passes by *my God.*" "Way" is the course of one's life; "justice" is a just cause or legal case that one might bring into court. The exiles were accusing God of exactly the same attitude and practice that they had been guilty of in the land of Judah, before the Exile. In the years just before the destruction of Jerusalem in 587 B.C., Jeremiah preached to the people, saying "If you truly practice justice (*mishpat*) between a man and his neighbor," implying of course that they had *not* been doing so, followed by a listing of their *un*just practices: oppression of the alien, orphan and widow; shedding of innocent blood; stealing; murder; adultery; false swearing in court (Jer 7:5–9). Now, how absurd for the exiles in Babylon to couple together the confession "The

---

[6]The Hebrew verb forms are in what modern grammarians call the durative imperfect, an action repeated again and again.

Lord . . . *my God*" with the accusation that God didn't care for them!

With his use of the names "Jacob . . . Israel," Isaiah is reminding the exiles that *their* God is the same God who made a covenant with Jacob/Israel long ago. He is the God who sees and knows, remembers and cares, and above all, acts on His people's behalf. Those exiles who knew the past well would recall to mind that at the first Exodus "the sons of Israel sighed because of the bondage, and they cried out and their cry for help . . . rose up to God. So God *heard* . . . and God *remembered* his covenant with Abraham, Isaac, and Jacob, and God *saw* and God *knew*" (Exod 2:23–25).

The Jewish exiles needed to grasp the vast truths of Isaiah's message about God (vv. 12–26), and *then* say " . . . *my* God."

40: 28–31. The Greatness of God

The greatness of God is summed up: He is "everlasting"—sovereign over time; He is "creator of the ends of the earth"—sovereign over space. But then, in an abrupt turn, Isaiah presents what at first appears to be a completely different God: all the vast energies of this incomparable God of verses 12–26 are available to the failing individual believer in need!

The chapter comes to a beautiful poetic conclusion, with wonderful words of encouragement to a depressed and discouraged people. They felt powerless. God had an abundance of power—and all of it was available for the weakest of them. They had but to "wait in hope for the Lord" and in the waiting,

> Will gain new strength;
> They will mount up with wings like eagles,

> They will run and not get tired,
> They will walk and not become weary (v. 31).

Several hundred years later, the first century A.D. missionary, Paul, would write: "We have this treasure in earthen vessels, that the surpassing greatness of the *power may be of God* and not from ourselves," and then in poetic-like praises sings:

> Afflicted in every way, but not crushed;
> Perplexed, but not despairing;
> Persecuted, but not forsaken;
> Struck down, but not destroyed (2 Cor 4:7–9).

We, too, must grasp both the greatness of God *and* His amazing condescension. We indeed may "run and not get tired." Why? Because *God* "does not become weary or tired." His strength is our strength!

IDOLS OF BABYLON, PRESENT YOUR CASE! (ISAIAH 41)

There are three major units in chapter 41:

- A Court Scene: with the Nations (vv. 1–7).
- Promises to God's Servant, Israel (vv. 8–20).
- A Court Scene: with the Deities of the Nations (vv. 21–29).

41:1–7. First Court Scene, with the Nations

Verses (41:) 1–4 focus on the *question before the court.* The Lord calls the nations ("the peoples," v. 1) to a great judicial contest. The "case" to be judged is: Who is the real power in history? The Lord or the gods of the nations? The "case" is to be "tried" in the context of the *headline news* of the day, news not only in Babylon, but reaching to the far distant "coastlands," the peoples residing in the westernmost extremities of the Babylonian Empire along the eastern Mediterranean Seacoast: *the phenomenally rapid rise to power of Cyrus of Persia,* "one from the east" of the Babylonian Empire.

The name, Cyrus the Persian, had been striking fear into the hearts of those in the world's seats of power for some years. Cyrus had been only a vassal king over the Persian kingdom of Anshan in southern Iran, subject to the powerful controlling Median Empire to the north. But revolt broke out in this Persian sector of the empire, and Cyrus was crowned king of Persia in the city of Pasargadae in 558 B.C. Only eight years later, in 550 B.C., Cyrus marched swiftly north, seized the Median capital city of Ecbatana, effectively taking over the vast Median Empire that stretched as far north and west as Armenia. This struck fear into the hearts of kings worldwide, and especially into that of Nabonidus (556—539 B.C.), ruler of the vast Babylonian Empire.[1] In an attempt to halt the spread of this Persian menace, Nabonidus entered into a mutual defense treaty with the kings of Egypt to the far southwest and of Lydia, a kingdom on the western extremity of Asia Minor (present-day Turkey). But it was all to no avail. In 547/6 B.C. Cyrus marched his army westward, sweeping across northern Mesopotamia, snatching that area from Babylonian control. He apparently also took Syria in northern Canaan and Cilicia in southeastern Asia Minor. Then, in the dead of winter, he crossed the Halys Mountains in central Asia Minor, attacked the Lydian capital, Sardis, by surprise, took it and brought Lydia into the Persian Empire. With Lydia gone, Babylon's defensive alliance with Egypt collapsed. Babylon stood alone.

Now, the primary question before Isaiah's imaginary "court" is: *Who has caused all this to happen?* (vv. 2, 4).

The sense of verse 2 would be best translated as a series of three questions:

> Who has aroused one from the east, calling him in righteousness to His service? [2]
> (Who) delivers up nations before him and subdues kings?

---

[1] Remember that Jerusalem had been destroyed in 587 B.C. by Babylonian king, Nebuchadnezzar. The Jews were already in exile in Babylonia by the time Cyrus came onto the world scene.

[2] "To his service," in the Hebrew is literally "to his feet." To be "in/to the feet" of someone is to be in one's service.

(Who) makes his sword like dust, his bow like wind-driven chaff?

The metaphors used in verse 2 express vividly the thoroughness and speed of Cyrus's victories and expansion of his empire. Verse 3 seems to imply that his rise to power was so effortless and swift that he seems to fly. But the sense of this verse is: "He pursues them. He passes by (in) peace (Heb., shalom) (on) a path his feet do not travel."

Cyrus did not gain all his empire by military force. There was a general discontent among the vassal kings of the Median Empire against their Median rulers. Many of them gave their loyalty, and their kingdoms, to Cyrus without a fight. Thus, there were paths his feet did not need to travel to gain war trophies. They came to him "in peace," and he dealt with them "in peace."

The question is now restated in verse 4: Who has done this? The question is widened to cover, not just the present historical/political situation, but "the generations from the beginning." That is, who has controlled the progress of history from the beginning of humankind?

The answer comes in the form of an emphatic statement: "I, the Lord, was [with] the first," that is, the first successful rulers in history's generations, and all since, and I am "with the last." Yes, "I am the one," who, from the beginning of history to the end of history, exists and directs all of history. It is I, the Lord, who "calls [Cyrus] in righteousness to His service."

Verses (41:) 5–7 picture the peoples of the distant nations, "coastlands," having heard of Cyrus's phenomenal success, calling an "international" conference to plan their strategy of defense. There is irony and comic drama here. Their strategy is to feverishly *build an idol* that will be more powerful than Cyrus' idol. The irony is that it was not *Cyrus'* gods they should fear, but *Israel's* God, the Lord, who is responsible for his success.

In the process each encourages the other, *"Be strong!"* First the craftsman/designer casts the idol image (see Isa 40:19). He, then, encourages the ones who must smelt, hammer and beat the gold for the gold plating to cover the image. Another solders the pieces together. The designer inspects the solder. "It is good," giving the *appearance* of solidity. The final irony is, as the Hebrew says, "he *strengthens* it with nails" and pronounces, "it will not totter." Of course it won't. It has been nailed to the floor! And here is the ultimate irony of idolatry: because the idol is nailed to the floor, immovable, it can do nothing for those who made it. The idol's appearance of solidity is only a figment of imagination.

It is only *the Lord* who cannot be moved and who brings stability into the chaotic conditions of nations at war. *His* "world is firmly established, it will not be moved," *His* "throne is established from of old," *His* "testimonies are fully confirmed" (Ps 93:1, 2, 5).

We, too, build our "idols" today. They may, indeed, be real idols. But for many they are the idols of economic success, the power of position, a network of relationships that benefits *me*, and more. *But our only stability is gained through faith in our unshakable God.* Oh, let us "turn from idols to serve a living and true God" (1 Thess. 1:9).

41:8-20. Promises to God's Servant, Israel

Verses (41:) 8–10 focus on God's command *that Israel is not to fear*. "But you, Israel" (v. 8) is in direct contrast to verse 5. The nations may fear, but Israel should not fear. Why? Because, says

God, "Israel [is] My servant." And Israel is a servant because she is "chosen." This speaks of *election*, but this passage illustrates a vital truth about the nature of election in biblical thought. Election is not for status and privilege, but for *servanthood and obedience*, and ultimately for the benefit of others.

Israel's fear was centered in her belief that, because she was now scattered to the "ends of the earth," to "its remotest parts," God had abandoned her. And there was certainly legitimate reason for abandonment: Israel's unfaithfulness. But God assures Israel that He has again "called" her from those very "ends of the earth," the very places from which "Abraham My friend" was called. And Israel is the "descendent" of Abraham, the very basis for a continued covenant relationship. With covenant language God assures them that he has *not* abandoned them: "*I am with you*" (v. 10), a formula with a long history, reaching back to Moses and the first Exodus ("I will be with you," Exodus 4:12; "It is . . . by Your going with us . . . that . . . . Your people may be distinguished from all the people who are upon the face of the earth," Exodus 33:16); "*I am your God*" (v. 10), likewise a formula with ancient roots in the first Exodus: "I am the Lord your God, who brought you out of the land of Egypt," (Exod 20:2; Deut 5:6). Fear is to be removed because of God's promises of strength, help and victory.

Verses (41:)11–16 promise *Israel's victory over her powerless enemies*. We find here a poetic weaving together of inverted themes (vv. 11–12). The hostility of their enemies is described in increasingly sharp terms. But just as their activity grows stronger to a climax, so their power wanes away to nothingness. That is, their actual power is *in inverse proportion* to their violence. This can be depicted as follows:

(a) Their Activity:

        (4) They "war with you" (actual warfare) (v. 12b)

      (3) They "quarrel with you" (physical assault) (v. 12a)

    (2) They "contend with you" (verbal opposition) (v. 11b)

  (1) They "are angered at you" (lit. "snort") (v. 11a)

(b) Their Impotence:

    (1) They "will be shamed and dishonored" (v. 11a)

    (2) They "will be as nothing and will perish" (v. 11b)

      (3, 4) they are "nonexistent" (12b)

What makes this possible? It is the supporting power of the Lord, who upholds *Israel's* right hand with *His* right hand (vv. 13 and 10). The right hand is the symbol of power and strength, yet Israel's right hand has lost its strength. But God's strength will be transferred to Israel, like the strength of a father becomes the strength of the child as hand grips hand.

And so powerless Israel's victory over her "powerful" enemies will not be at all due to Israel's greatness, for they are nothing but a "worm" (v. 14). God is sometimes so astonishingly blunt! But a "Redeemer" (Heb., *go'el*) will come to their assistance.

A *go'el* was a male kinsman-protector. His functions were mainly three: (1) to avenge the death of a relative (e.g., Num 35:12), (2) to buy back mortgaged land or enslaved relatives (e.g., Lev 25:23), and (3) to carry on the name and inheritance of a dead relative (e.g., the story of Ruth and Boaz). Thus, the term *go'el* carries the sense of Protector, Defender, Champion, and Deliverer. He is one who protects the interests of his relatives by every means in his power.

Thus, to call the Lord, Israel's Redeemer suggests that the Lord's covenant bond with Israel was as strong as any human bond of blood and kinship. The idea of God as Redeemer was already firmly associated with the first Exodus (e.g., Exod 6:6; 15:13; Isa 51:10; Ps. 74:2; Ps. 106:10). What the Lord is promising to do for the Exiles in Babylon, then, will be another Exodus, again with Himself as Redeemer.

Verses 15–16 present another vivid metaphor, a powerful "threshing sledge." A threshing sledge was like a flat wooden platform without wheels or runners. Rather, bits of sharp iron or stone were set in the bottom. After the grain had been harvested and gathered to the threshing floor, the farmer rode on his threshing sledge while his oxen pulled it back and forth over the grain, cutting it to tiny bits, preparing it for winnowing on a windy day.

Now, the question is, *who* is the threshing sledge here? The Hebrew syntax in verses 15–16 allows for two possible translations: (1) "I have made you a . . . threshing sledge," or (2) "had I made you a . . . threshing sledge," in the sense of "*if* I had made you . . . ." The second best fits the overall sense of the whole passage, so that we would translate as follows:

> If I had made you a sharp threshing sledge, new, with double edges
> You would thresh the mountains, and pulverize (them), and you would make the hills like chaff.
> You would winnow them, and the wind would carry them away, and the storm would scatter them.[3]

[3] See John D. W. Watts, *Word Biblical Commentary: Isaiah 34–66* (Waco, Texas: Word Books, Publisher, 1987) p. 107.

Indeed, the Lord *could* have made exiled Israel the threshing sledge, to do the work that Cyrus is now doing—cutting to bits the political and military powers of the earth. And if He had, Israel would take to herself all the glory of the victory. But the point is that God *has not* done so. Rather than wage war (He appoints others to do this), the Lord insists that Israel's calling is to be a very different one: "You will *rejoice* **in** the Lord, **In** the Holy One of Israel you shall *sing praises*" (v. 16b).

"Sing praises" is better here, not "glory" as in some translations. And Israel was to sing praises *in,* not *to* the Lord. Praise is not simply directed toward Him. *He is the basis, the reason for our praise!* Here is an Old Testament parallel to the New Testament usage of the term "in Christ," "in the Lord," "in the Spirit" (e.g., Eph 1:1; 5:10; 6:18).

Verses (41:) 17–20 continue Isaiah's theme of reversal with the *promise that the desert will be transformed into an oasis.* The word pictures ("seeking water," "parched with thirst," "dry land," "desert") anticipate the hardship of the journey back to Judah from Babylon, but also hold out the promise of divine, supernatural provision along the way ("rivers, "springs," "fountains"). Again, here is an echo of the Exodus-Wilderness theme.

Praise (see the comment on v. 16b) is often mentioned in relation to God's gracious provision, as here, for the "poor and needy" (v. 17). "Poor" and "needy" is a frequent combination of terms. Such people were always the special concern of the Lord, as David assumes when he pleads:

> Since I am poor and needy,
> The Lord is mindful of me;
> You are my help and my deliverer;
> Do not delay, O my God (Ps 40:17).

36

The poor and needy were often defined as the alien/stranger, the orphan, and the widow (see Lev 19:10 with Deut 24:17-21; see also Jer. 7:6).

Israel's complaint that she is "needy" (v.17) is legitimate. Exiled Israel is indeed an *alien* in a foreign land; she is indeed like a *widow*, for she has been bereft of her "husband," the Lord, or so it appears. But just as in the time before the first Exodus, when enslaved Israel's "cry for help . . .rose up to God . . .and God heard their groaning" (Exod 2:23-24), so now the Lord insists that, "I, the Lord, answer them; As God of Israel, I do not forsake them" (v. 17).

God's promise of direct, personal assistance (vv. 18-19) may be interpreted in historical, eschatological and figurative contexts.

In the *historical* context, God provides "water" in abundance when there is no water and His people are parched with thirst, as in the first Exodus. Near the end of their forty-year journey, poised on the eastern side of the Jordan, Moses reminded Israel that "[God] led you through the great and terrible wilderness, with its fiery serpents and scorpions and thirsty ground where there was no water; he brought water for you out of the rock of flint" (Deut 8:15; see Exod 17:6). Now, God can and will do so again for these exiled Jews on their difficult journey back to Judah from Babylon, in this coming second Exodus.

In the *eschatological* context, we may allow here for the vision of the actual transformation of nature in the final redemption and return of God's people in the new creation, where water sources and luxuriant forests appear in the barren and desolate "wilderness." We may link this passage with Isaiah's earlier word in chapter 35:

> The wilderness and the desert will be glad,

37

And the Arabah will rejoice and blossom;
Like the crocus it will blossom profusely
And rejoice with rejoicing and shout for joy (vv. 1–2).

And the ransomed of the Lord will return,
And come with joyful shouting to Zion,
With everlasting joy upon their heads.
They will find gladness and joy,
And sorrow and sighing will flee away (v. 10).

Figuratively, God's promise is to any of us who, in life's dry situations, feel like the bare sun-baked desert, cut off from all sources of renewal, to any of us who, like Ezekiel, feel that "our bones are dried up, and our hope has perished" (Ezek 37:11). The Lord remains able to open up "springs in the desert" and bring spiritual refreshment to our innermost beings.

But God's "answer" (v. 17) is not merely that His people may drink when thirsty, that life may be sustained, but that "they may see and know" (v. 20). But "they" is ambiguous. Is it Israel or the peoples of the world who are to "know"?

"Knowing" is exactly what Isaiah has earlier said Israel is not capable of doing:

An ox knows its owner,
And a donkey its master's manger,
But Israel does not know,
My people do not understand (Isa 1:3; see also 6:9).

The literal translation of the second line of verse 20 is: "[that] they may position and understand [them] together." "Position" (Heb., *sim*) often speaks of God "assigning, placing" things or events. If "they" is Israel, then Israel is being challenged to put/position into proper perspective the things she has experienced, to "understand (them) together." That is, if she can think of her remarkable survival through the past years of exile and God's new call to liberation (40:9–11) in terms of the Lord's plans and actions, she will be in a position to rejoice and sing the praises of verse 16.

But if "they" means the peoples of the world, then the actual return of the Jews to Judah would be a sign to them of the power of Israel's God and His action in history. The ultimate purpose of Israel's salvation would be the peoples' acknowledgement of the Lord as the only God.

In either case, or both, Isaiah's use of the term "know" is again a link with the first Exodus, where the ultimate purpose of God's saving of Israel from Egypt was that Pharaoh, the Egyptians and the Israelites would "know" who was truly and solely God (see Exod 6:7; 7:5; 7:17; 8:10, 22; 9:14; 14:4, 18, 31; compare also Ezekiel's use of the expression, "Then you shall know that I am the Lord," Ezek 6:10, 13, 14; 36:23, 38; 37:13, and more).

"That the hand of the Lord has done this, and the Holy One of Israel has created it" (v. 20) summarizes the basis of Isaiah's theology. In chapters 1–39 Isaiah looks at Israel's history from the 8th century onward, including Assyria's rise and subsequent invasions of Israel and Judah, resulting in Samaria's capture, Assyria's fall and the rise of Babylon, resulting in Jerusalem's destruction, and now (from chapter 40) the rise of Persia. Isaiah concludes that the Lord planned all this and carried it out—*Isaiah* sees the Lord's plan and purpose in history and calls upon the Jews of the Exile to do the same.

But this message and call is not only for the Jews of the Exile, but for believers of all times and places. It is for us, today, in our modern, twenty-first century world. We are called to look at the flow of historical events in the nations around us, and "know" and "understand" that "the hand of the Lord has done this"!

41:21–29. Second Court Scene, with the Deities of the Nations

Verses (41:) 21–24 focus on *the powerlessness of the deities.* The issue here is the ability to both predict events and to bring them about as predicted. Isaiah becomes sarcastic. These deities cannot tell about the future. Can they tell us about the past? No? Can they do something good, or bad? No? Well, then, can they say "Boo!" and scare us? The overwhelming answer to the questions is: they are "nothing" and their "work amounts to nothing" (v. 24).

Verses (41:) 25–29 declare that *the Lord controls events.* Here, the Lord, Himself, predicts a future event, the coming of a new conqueror. The main issue before the court (seen in 41:1–7) is the phenomenal rise of Cyrus. The Lord's claim is that he alone, not the gods of the nations, is responsible for this: "*I* stirred up one . . ." This "one" (Cyrus) is coming "from the north" and "from the rising of the sun" (i.e., the east; see comments on Isa 41:1–4). The Lord then throws out a question to the nations' deities: "Who has declared . . . ." That is, who among you gods has ever declared a thing? And the answer is: Not one of you. In fact, no one has ever even heard you speak!

The final verdict of the court, then, is that the gods of the nations and their idols are "nothing," "worthless," simply "wind and emptiness" (v. 29). At the same time, the case is decided in favor of the Lord: He not only *predicts* a future event, but he also *produces* and *controls* that event. Therefore, only He is truly God!

JUSTICE TO THE NATIONS (ISAIAH 42)

There are three major units in chapter 42:

- ❑ The Servant of the Lord (First "Servant Song") (vv. 1–9).
- ❑ A Song of Praise to the Lord the Warrior (vv. 10–17).
- ❑ Israel: God's Disobedient Servant (vv. 18–25).

42:1–9. (First "Servant Song") The Servant of the Lord

Isaiah introduces to us a figure who is called "My Servant" (v. 1). The form of the introduction is as though this "Servant" is already present (v. 1), but whose mission and its ultimate fulfillment lie in the future (v. 4).

This is the first of the four "Servant Songs" (the other three are Isa 48:1–7; 50:4–11; 52:13–53:12). In these songs, the "servant" reference is rather clearly to an individual figure. *But,* there are several other references to *Israel* as a servant, in a corporate sense (for example, Isa 41:8–10; 42:18–25; 43:10; 44:1–5; 44:21). So, here in Isaiah 42:1, we are immediately faced with a question of identity: *Who is this Servant?*

One possibility, within the overall context, is that the servant is Cyrus, the Persian king. Yes, Cyrus would be a deliverer; he would give Israel freedom from Babylon; he was the agent of God himself (he is even called the Lord's "Shepherd" (Isa 44:28) and "anointed" (Isa 45:1). But God's ultimate purposes for His beloved people—the new exodus, the new creation, redemption—would need more than a Persian Cyrus.

Thus, we are introduced to this Servant—a deliverer very different and superior to Cyrus. But, who is he? It is rather clear that he is an individual who was yet in the future from the prophet's point of view. From the historical viewpoint of the New Testament, we see this Servant as the messianic figure fulfilled in Jesus Christ. But the text of Isaiah does not tell us this. Our immediate concern, therefore, should be: what is the nature of his character and mission?

Verses (42:) 1–4 depict *the Servant's endowment and mission.* The Lord, Himself, is the speaker. The form of the speech is that of public announcement, similar to the formal announcement of the coronation of a king (compare Ps. 2:7). The Lord uses three verbs about His Servant (v. 1): "uphold," meaning held fast by God to do His will; "chosen"; "delights," that is, accepts favorably. Furthermore, the Lord says, "I have put My Spirit upon him." This speaks of total dependence upon God. "The Spirit" was also a prominent feature of Isaiah's earlier vision of the messianic son of David, the "shoot" or "branch" that was to spring from the "stem of Jesse" (Isa 11:1–2). There is probably an intentional linking of the two ideas, that is, the Servant has some of the features of a *king* (chosen by God, anointed by the Spirit, custodian of law and justice). But his mission is described in terms that more resemble a *prophet.*

His mission is stated three times in similar terms: "He will bring forth *justice* to the nations" (v. 1); "He will faithfully bring forth *justice*" (v. 3); "Until He has established *justice* in the earth" (v. 4).

What is the meaning of "justice" here? The Hebrew term *mishpat* (justice) is used in three basic contexts: (1) legal judgments and ordinances (as in Exod 21–23); (2) all the

42

practicalities of daily life in accordance with God's desire, that is, not merely legal affairs; (3) the social requirements of the covenant relationship since Abraham (Gen 18:19), and especially since the Sinai experience. Thus, "justice" includes true faith in the living, covenant God, plus right action among one's fellow human beings on earth.

Justice is also linked with "law," Hebrew *torah* (v. 4), which has a similar meaning: guidance for living a life ethically acceptable to God in the light of His revelation. This combination of "justice" and "law" in the mission of the Lord's Servant casts him also in the role of a *new Moses,* who had originally mediated these things to Israel. Moses was prophet, leader and also the model "servant of the Lord" (Num 12:7).

With the use of seven negatives (vv. 2–3) a deliberate contrast is made between this Servant and other kinds of leaders. His mission will not be accomplished by personal force or political power, but rather by quiet and compassionate service. His justice will be gentle, not harsh and rough (v. 3). He will exercise a ministry of restoration to the "bruised reed" and "dimly burning wick" (v. 3), an apparent reference to the exiles themselves.

There is an interesting wordplay here. "Disheartened or crushed" (v. 4) are from the same Hebrew roots as "reed" and "wick" (v. 3). Just as God's people in exile will not be snuffed out, so the Servant will complete his task without being snuffed out. He and his rule of justice will not be a failure!

But the Servant's mission is not merely to Israel. The "coastlands," the western extremities of Isaiah's known world, representing all mankind, near and far, "wait expectantly for His law" (v. 4). Later, Isaiah says that the coastlands are waiting for God, Himself (Isa 51:5), thus identifying the mission of the Servant with the mission of God, Himself, in the world.

Thus, Isaiah is not talking about Cyrus for the needs of Israel, but the Servant for the whole of mankind.

Verses (42:) 5–9 describe *the Servant's calling.* We are immediately faced with the question: To whom is this portion of the Lord's speech addressed? Who is the "you" to whom the Lord says,

> I have called you in righteousness,
> I will also hold you by the hand and watch over you,
> And I will appoint you as a covenant to the people (v. 6)?

Some say it is Cyrus, who was "called in righteousness" (Isa 45:13; compare Isa 46:11; 48:15). We might see Cyrus bringing "out prisoners . . . those who dwell in darkness from the prison" (Isa 42:7)—that is, the Jewish exiles from Babylon—but it is difficult to see how he could be "a covenant to the people," or a "light to the nations" (Isa 42:6). Some say it is Israel. The first line of verse 6 does echo what was said about Israel as a whole in Isaiah 41:9, but it is difficult to see how Israel "opens blind eyes" or "brings out prisoners" (v. 7). Therefore, it is best to take these verses as addressed to *the individual Servant figure* described in Isaiah 42:1–4.

Verse 5 is a hymnic introduction, emphasizing the status of the One who commissions the Servant. This One is not merely one of the many Babylonian national deities, such as god Bel or god Nebo, whom Isaiah discounts as being no gods at all, but "God the Lord,"

> Who created the heavens and stretched them out,
> Who spread out the earth and its vegetation,
> Who gives breath to the people on it,
> And spirit to those who walk in it.

This world belongs to God the Lord! And because of this, it is into *God's* world that the Servant is being sent. The Servant will not be dependent merely upon His own resources. Rather, His strength and encouragement to carry out His mission lie in God Himself.

The Servant has been called "in righteousness" (v. 6). In Isaiah, righteousness and salvation are often used in parallel and thus are almost synonymous in meaning. For example,

> Let the earth open up and *salvation* bear fruit,
> And *righteousness* spring up with it (Isa 45:8; also 46:13; 51:6, 8)

Thus, we could translate the first line of Isaiah 41:6 as, "I have called you for my saving purpose."

Moreover, the Servant is appointed "as a covenant to the people" (v. 6). "People" is in parallel with "nations," thus refers to all the peoples of the earth. Isaiah, then, envisions the role of the Servant in extending the covenant relationship that exists between God and Israel to all the rest of mankind. This is, then, *a universal vision,* an ultimate fulfillment of the Lord's promise to Abraham: "In you all the families of the earth shall be blessed" (Gen 12:3).

The release of "prisoners" and "those who dwell in darkness" (v. 7), as a further part of the Servant's mission has two implications. It refers to the literal release of the exiles from their Babylonian captivity. But also, in the universal context of verses 5–6, it can be applied to liberation from all bondage that afflicts mankind—physical, social and spiritual.

But perhaps the Jewish exiles in Babylon may ask, "Does God have the power to carry out this worldwide plan through His Servant?" Can He bring it to pass? And God's answer through His prophet Isaiah is that the people can know that God will fulfill this plan because He has fulfilled His plans

before. He has already shown that He is the God who speaks
and then acts.

> See, the former things have come to pass,
> Now I declare new things;
> Before they begin to happen
> I make them known to you (Isa 42:9).

The "former things," at least in part, refer to Israel's
experience of God throughout the time of her national existence
before the Exile. Prophets of the Lord appeared regularly to
declare what God has been doing, was presently doing, and was
going to do. For instance, in the eighth century, Isaiah himself
had warned Judean kings Ahaz and Hezekiah that the Assyrians
would invade Judah, but that they (the Assyrians), and other
contemporary powers would eventually see their own downfall.
His words had come true. Some of his words were coming true
before the exiles' own eyes: Babylon was about to fall at the
hand of the Medes[1], as Isaiah had said:

> Behold, I am going to stir up the Medes against them . . .
> And Babylon, the beauty of kingdoms,
> The glory of the Chaldean's pride,
> Will be as when God overthrew Sodom and Gomorrah
> (Isa 13:17-19).

In the notes on Isa 42:1-9 we said that from the historical
viewpoint of the New Testament, we see this Servant as the
messianic figure ultimately fulfilled in Jesus Christ. Yes, Jesus is
the Servant *par excellence.* Yet, earlier, Isaiah had reminded the
exiles that Israel was also called to be God's servant. God's

---

[1] Though Cyrus was a Persian, he had conquered the Median territory
to the north, and joined their armies with his. Thus, the Medes and the
Persians had come to be nearly synonymous.

purpose was to reach the world through Israel. But Israel had failed to "bring light to the nations." So, it is Jesus who is the light of the world, He who brings a covenant relationship with His Father into which all peoples may enter. Jesus' fulfillment of the servant's calling is not the end of its significance, however, for as well as saying of Himself, "I am the light of the world" (John 8:12), He also said to His followers, "You are the light of the world" (Matt 5:14), and "As the Father has sent me, I also send you" (John 20:21). Jesus, then, returns the servant calling to the people of God to whom it first belonged.

42:10–17. A Song of Praise to the Lord the Warrior

God's new plan of action requires a "new song" (v. 10). In this song (vv. 10–17) Isaiah adopts the three-part hymnic style seen in several Psalms: (1) A summons to praise; (2) Glorification of the Lord as world-creator, or victor over other nations and their gods, or other acts of God on behalf of Israel; (3) Announcement of the Lord's coming as Judge of the world. (For comparison, take time to read through Psalm 33, a song of praise and thanks to the Lord who created and preserves, and Psalms 96, 98 and 149, all songs of praise to the Lord as King.)

Verses (42:) 10–12 are a universal summons to sing praise to the Lord, even "from the end of the world." This summons fits well with Isaiah's overall references to the universal scope of God's new plan of action. The universalness of the summons is seen in the extremities of Isaiah's world. "The coastlands" (v. 12) are the lands bordering the Mediterranean Sea to the west (v. 10). "Kedar" (v. 11) is the desert east of Israel, and "Sela" (v. 11) a city in the southeast extremity. So, it is not merely to Israel—in fact, perhaps not to Israel at all—that the summons rings out, but to all peoples when they see what God is doing for His enslaved people. Even creation is called to join in the praise as seen in Isaiah's call to "all that is in the sea" and "you islands" (v. 10), and "the wilderness" (v. 11). Here, Isaiah reflects the Psalmists' theme of all creation rejoicing at God's intervention in the affairs of men. Note the Psalmists' call to the *heavens,* the *earth,* the *sea,* the *field,* the *trees,* the *rivers,* and the *mountains* to *be glad, rejoice, thunder, exult, sing for joy,* and *clap their hands* (Ps 96:11–12; 98:7–8).

Verses (42:) 13–15 cast the Lord in two seemingly contrasting figures. The first is as a "man of war" or "mighty warrior," who "utters a [battle] shout" and "raises a war cry," who "prevails against His enemies" (v. 13). Isaiah draws this figure for the Lord from the old tradition of the Exodus, seen most vividly in the song of Moses and Israel, sung on the eastern side of the Red Sea "when Israel saw the great power which the Lord had used against the Egyptians" (Exod 14:31). Note Moses' description of the Lord in Exodus 15: "The Lord is a warrior" (v. 3), "Your right hand, O Lord, shatters the enemy" (v. 6), "You overthrow those who rise up against You, You send forth Your burning anger, and it consumes them as chaff" (v. 7).

Thus Isaiah presents the Lord as victor over all enemies. Such a figure is in strong contrast with the atmosphere of the Servant Song seen just previously (Isa 42:1–9). The picture of violent rage and destruction is set alongside the gentle and compassionate nature of the Servant. (Even more blood-stained will be the figure seen later in Isa 63:1–6.) But we must see both truths in Scripture: the One who suffers for His people, and the mighty conquering victor. We must then relate them both ultimately to what actually did fulfill both: the ministry, death and resurrection of Jesus. C.R. North comments:

Our Incomparable God

It was natural for the Hebrews to assume that when God visited the world in judgment there would be carnage: blood would be shed. When he did come, in the Incarnation, blood was shed; but it was man, not God, who shed it, and the blood that was shed was not man's, but the blood of the incarnate Son of God . . . . The Hebrews firmly believed that God is personal; they could never think of him as indifferent to the fate of the world. He would act . . . . He did act, but in a very different way from what was expected of him (see John 3:17). We might call this the 'inverse' fulfillment of prophecy.[2]

The second figure is that of "a women in labor," groaning, gasping and panting (v. 14). From having been quiet and peaceful, she suddenly starts to cry and shout and move violently. God says He has "kept silent" and "restrained" Himself. Isaiah uses these same terms in his later collective song of lament, perhaps repeating the complaint of the Exiles themselves, that God is silent and does not answer prayer:

Will you *restrain* Yourself at these things, O Lord?
Will you *keep silent* and afflict us beyond measure? (Isa 64:12).

The two figures, though different—the one, male bringing death, the other, female bringing forth life—make the same point: as the warrior *suddenly* goes into battle, and the pregnant woman *suddenly* begins to give birth, so will God, after His

---

[2] Christopher R. North, *The Second Isaiah; Introduction, Translation, and Commentary to Chapters XL-LV* (Oxford: Clarendon Press, 1964) p. 116. I do not agree with the assumption that the title of North's book implies, that a second "Isaiah" wrote chapters 40–55. I do, however, find his comments on this present passage to be commendable.

silence for a season, suddenly act now that He is setting out to rescue His people.

The destructive power of God's action "wastes" and "withers" everything in its path. Verse 15 is in contrast to Isaiah 41:18–20, where God turns the desert into fertile land. Here is the reverse action. But Psalm 107:33–37 portrays these as opposite sides of the same act; for example, "He changes rivers into a wilderness . . . . He changes a wilderness into a pool of water" (Ps 107:33–34). The intent of both actions is that the "wise" should "consider the lovingkindnesses of the Lord" (Ps 107:43).

Verses (42:) 16–17 speak of the " blind" (v. 16), the Jewish Exiles, who could no longer see the greatness of God. And the cause of their blindness is *idol worship*. In shame, the Exiles have turned their backs on the Lord, just as Israel had done long before at the foot of Mt. Sinai, when Aaron declared to them concerning the golden calf idol: "This is your god, O Israel" (Exod 32:4).[3] And, because they cannot see the "way" or "paths" to walk, God will "lead" them by the hand. "Way" carries both literal and metaphorical implications here: literal, in that God would lead Israel back across the wilderness to Judah; metaphorical in the sense of the right way, that is, back into a true ethical relationship with Himself. And as God leads them along, His presence, who Himself is "light" (1 John 1:5;

---

[3] Isaiah 42:17, when literally translated, reads: "They have turned backwards. They are totally shamed who are trusting in the idol (singular), who are saying to an image (singular), 'You (plural) are our gods.'" Exodus 32:4 literally reads, "These (plural) are your gods (plural). Isaiah here appears to deliberately use the plural to link this new act of God with the old Exodus.

compare John 1:4–5; 8:12; 9:5), will push back the "darkness."
And God will perform a miracle: He will put within His
spiritually deaf and blind people the ability to hear and see
(Isa 42:18), as we will see in the next segment of our study.

42:18–25, Israel, God's Disobedient Servant

"Blind" (v. 18) is the keyword linking this section with the
previous one (vv. 10–17). Possibly this is God's reply to His
people who have been accusing *Him* of being deaf and blind to
their captivity. The implied question is: "Who is really blind
here, I or you?"

"Hear, you deaf! And look, you blind! that you may see"
(v. 18) is, in itself, a command to faith, an appeal for a miracle.
Why tell the deaf to hear and the blind to see, unless God is
going to give them the ability to do so?

Verse 20 again picks up the servant language. "My servant"
in this context is Israel as a people in their present state of
captivity. The Lord had chosen Israel to be a servant and a
messenger, but present blindness and deafness make such
service impossible.

Israel's condition of blindness and deafness was not
accidental, but the result of a willful disobedience (v. 20).
Though their eyes and ears are open, they have *refused* to
"observe" and "hear." Earlier Isaiah had said:

> For this is a rebellious people, false sons,
> Sons who *refuse* to listen
> To the instruction (Heb., Torah) of the Lord (Isa 30:9).

In a very real sense the Exiles have become like the idols in
which they have come to trust (Isa 42:17), idols, which, in the
words of the Psalmist,

> Have eyes, but they cannot see;

51

> They have ears, but they cannot hear (Ps 115:5–6).

The Psalmist realistically adds:

> Those who make them [i.e., idols] will become like them,
> Everyone who trusts in them (Ps 115:8).

Verses (42:)21–22 must be seen together. "The Law" (Heb., *Torah*, v. 21) is a reference to God's revelation of His "great and glorious" gift of grace to an enslaved people in Egypt, through the spoken and written word of Moses, making them His distinctive people. As God's distinctive people, redeemed out of Egypt, Israel was called to mediate God's saving blessing to all nations. Note Moses' words to Israel on the eve of their entrance into Canaan:

> See, I have taught you statutes and judgments just as the Lord my God commanded me . . . So keep and do them, for that is your wisdom and your understanding in the sight of the peoples who will hear all these statutes and say, "Surely this great nation is a wise and understanding people" . . . what great nation is there that has statutes and judgments as righteous as this whole law (Heb., Torah) which I am setting before you today? (Deut 4:5–8; see also Exod 19:3–6).

But the present plight of Israel—"plundered," "despoiled," "trapped," hidden away," "a prey" (v. 22)—is in stark contrast to God's intention for them.

What was the cause of their present plight? Was it merely fate? No. Was it because Babylon was stronger than Israel? No. Rather, it was a definite act of the Lord Himself against His own people, in judgment for their sins ("Who gave Jacob up . . .? Was it not the Lord . . .?" v. 24)). "They were not willing" (v. 24) links this section of Isaiah's prophecy with an earlier word:

> For thus the Lord God, the Holy One of Israel, has said,
> "In repentance and rest you shall be saved,
> In quietness and trust is your strength."
> But you were not willing (Isa 30:15).

It was in the "ways" of the Lord that Israel had not been willing to walk. This explains further why God's people did not "know" and were "blind" to the "way," mentioned in the previous section (Isa 42:16). But the basic problem is that "They did not obey [God's] law (Heb., *Torah*)" (v. 24).

The sum of it all is, they *did not want to hear or obey.* God's judgment followed—"the heat of His anger . . .the fierceness of battle . . .aflame all around"—yet, in her spiritual stubbornness, Israel "did not take it to heart" (v. 25).

A Summary of the "Servant" Theology Up to This Point

The first picture of the servant is a corporate figure—Israel herself. Israel has been chosen—as descendants of Abraham and as recipients of God's *Justice* and *Law* (Heb., *Mishpat* and *Torah)*. This points to Israel as God's intended model or pattern. By their obedience and commitment to Him and His covenant requirements, God intended that they show the rest of the world God's true pattern for humanity (see Gen 18:18–19; Exod 19:3–6). Israel, as God's servant, was to be "a light to the nations" (Isa 49:6).

The significance of Israel, therefore, lies as much in what they *were* (or were called *to be*), as in the message they carried. This is what makes so relevant the whole social structure and life of Israel. *Their mission was to be a certain kind of people in the midst of the world!*

53

So far, however, we have seen in our study that Israel was failing in this mission. Israel's failure, in spite of knowing God's Justice and Law, had been what had led to the judgment of the Exile. Corporately, Israel was a failed servant—blind and deaf. She has the status of servant, but not the spiritual sight and hearing necessary to one who is to be God's messenger. She has sight, but not insight. The Lord wanted to commend His revelation to the world. The way of doing that was to show how well it worked in Israel. But in fact it did not work at all in Israel, because she would not take it seriously. Therefore, God cannot fulfill His purpose through Israel.

The second picture of the servant is of the individual figure—distinct from Israel, with ultimate fulfillment in Jesus Christ. The same language is used of Him. The same role is given to Him: service to the whole of mankind, to bring redemption, justice and liberation. He takes on the role that was originally Israel's.

Yet the total content of the Servant's mission, as given by Isaiah—justice, liberation, peace, restoration—was certainly not exhausted in Jesus' earthly ministry. How then? The Church is entrusted with His mission, both in proclamation and presence. *Our mission is to be a certain kind of people in the midst of the world!* The Lord wants to commend His revelation to the world. His only way of doing so is to show how well it works in His Church—in *us!* Do we take this commission seriously? *Can* God fulfill his purpose through us?

FEAR NOT! I HAVE REDEEMED YOU
(ISAIAH 43)

There are four major units in chapter 43:

- ❑ Israel Redeemed and Repatriated (vv. 1–7).
- ❑ Israel as God's Witnesses (vv. 8–13).
- ❑ The Fall of Babylon and a New Exodus (vv. 14–21).
- ❑ Israel's Sin and the Lord's forgiveness (vv. 22–28)..

Chapter 42 closed with the depiction of a servant (Israel) who, by God's call and commission, was supposed to bring sight to the blind and freedom to the prisoner, but who, by his own stubborn willfulness, is sightless and himself a prisoner. The natural response is for God to turn His back on such an unworthy servant. In three ways, however, God says "No" to this response: "No," because I still love him; "No," because I still intend him to be my servant; "No," because I am going to restore him.

43:1–7. Israel redeemed and Repatriated

Verses (40:) 1–3. "But now" (v. 1) closely links this section with the message at the end of chapter 42—Yes, your past and your present are dark, lying under God's judgment on your sin. *But,* this is what God is *now* saying to you for the future . . .

"Created" (v. 7) or "Creator," (v. 1), "formed" (v. 1) and "made" (v. 7) are all "Genesis" words for creation. In this section (vv. 1–7) creation language is paired off with the theme of redeeming and calling, thus combining the two most prominent themes in the Old Testament, Creation and Redemption. As Israel's "Creator" and "Shaper" ("He who formed you;" the verb is used to describe the work of a potter shaping a vessel), God has a rightful claim upon Israel.

"Fear not . . . ." This divine command is used often in Scripture to signal an impending change from the present, negative circumstance, to something new and positive (see, for example, Gen 15:1; 21:17; 26:24). In Israel's present circumstance, it signals the impending canceling of old, present guilt and the announcement of a new era of salvation and blessing.

Three reasons are given for Israel not to fear. (1) "I have redeemed you" (v. 1). This is a reference to the former Exodus when God brought Israel out of Egyptian bondage. This is also God's second rightful claim upon Israel. (2) "I have called your name" (v. 1), that is, I have *named* you. A parent, usually the father, who begets a child, names that child. Such naming signifies that the child is *his.* (3) "You are Mine" (v. 1), signifying close family relationship. In giving these three reasons, God is affirming, "Oh, Israel, my beloved, what I have done in the past, I will do again. Don't fear . . . ."

"Water" and "fire" (v. 2) are symbols of extreme danger (see Ps. 66:12). Israel will be harmed by neither. The promise here refers to protection on the return journey from Babylon to Judah. It promises protection *in the midst* of danger, not *out* of danger. There are echoes here of the personal assurances of protection of Psalms 91 and 121. God can make such promises because he is Lord of all natural forces (a point already made in Isa 40:12, 22–26). This metaphor also contrasts the future with the past. In Isaiah 42:25, Israel is being burned in God's judgment (past). But in Isaiah 43:2, Israel will *not* be burned, because of God's redemption (future).

Redemption usually requires the payment of a "ransom," something given in the place of the one redeemed. Here, the Lord says He has given (already decided, though it is still future) "Egypt," "Cush" and "Seba" as Israel's "ransom" (v. 3). This would include all of Egypt, Ethiopia and Sudan, representing all of Africa as then known to the Jews. The idea here seems to be that God would allow Cyrus, whom God had summoned to facilitate Israel's return to her homeland in Judah and to Jerusalem, to have "Africa" as a bonus. This would be more than had ever previously been conquered by the empires from the east. God would give this in exchange for the liberation of Israel and the restoration of Jerusalem. In historical fact, it was Cambyses, Cyrus' successor, who successfully conquered Egypt and brought it into the Persian Empire.

Verse (43:) 4 gives one of the most beautiful and profound statements of the biblical concept of election. "You are precious in my sight" echoes and confirms the earlier classic statement of Israel's election:

> I bore you on eagles' wings, and brought you to Myself. Now then, if you will indeed obey My voice and keep My covenant, then you shall be My own possession among all the peoples, for all the earth is Mine; and you shall be to Me a kingdom of priests and a holy nation (Exod 19:4-6).

Israel is the people to whom God has turned in "love." They, just as they are, are dear and precious in His sight. So precious, in fact, that God says, "I give (of) mankind in exchange for you" (v. 4), a restatement of the ransom promise in verse 3. God is manipulating historical forces in Persia and Egypt—all *for the sake of tiny Israel,* His beloved people.

57

Verses (43:) 5–7 refer to the scattered Exiles of other deportations also. There will be an ingathering of God's people from the four corners of the earth—"east," "west," "north," "south"—a united, restored Israel. This was also the prophetic vision of Jeremiah and Ezekiel. For example,

> "Days are coming," declares the Lord, "when it will no longer be said, 'As the Lord lives, who brought up the sons of Israel out of the land of Egypt,' but, 'As the Lord lives, who brought up the sons of Israel from the land of the north and from all the countries where He had banished them.' for I will restore them to their own land" (Jer. 16:14–15),

Or,

> I will bring them out from the peoples and gather them from the countries, and bring them to their own land (Ezek 34:13).

But Isaiah's vision of the ingathering, of the restoration here must be understood rightly. This return fits the pattern of Isa 2:1–4 and 66:18–21. There is no promise here of return to political power. The intention is that Israel become the spiritual servant she was called to be, to whom

> All the nations will stream.
> And many peoples will come and say,
> 'Come, let us go up to the mountain of the Lord,
> To the house of the God of Jacob;
> That He may teach us concerning His ways,
> And that we may walk in His paths' (Isa 2:22–23).

Or,

> I will set a sign among them and will send survivors from them to the nations . . .that have neither heard My fame nor seen My glory. And they will declare My glory among the nations (Isa 66:19).

Verse 7 is a succinct description of Israel, in their origin, their role and their destiny: "for God's glory." This is still true of the People of God at all times!

43:8–13. Israel as God's Witnesses

This passage again takes up the theme of a hypothetical trial (as in Isa 41:1–5 and Isa 41:21–29). This time both Israel and all the nations of the earth are called to be present. The question before the "court", however, is still the same: who is truly God, the Lord or the gods of the nations? But this time the purpose of the trial is not to convince the nations, but to convince *Israel!*

To this trial witnesses are summoned. The one to appear on the Lord's behalf is Israel. The other deities are to produce witnesses from among the nations. The evidence to be produced concerns "former things" (v. 9): a deity's spoken message, a proclamation (word), demonstrated in event (act). That is, are there any former events that the nations' deities have foretold and which have actually taken place? Are there any witnesses among the nations who have publicly heard such foretelling and have actually experienced their fulfilling? The irony is that, since the deities of the nations are both unable to speak and lifeless, they cannot call any witnesses. And if they are unable to speak, they certainly could not have made any proclamations. Yet, the Lord, who is both living and speaks, is able to call witnesses—Israel.

Verse (43:) 8 presents a paradox about the Lord's witnesses (the same as in Isa 42:18–21): they possess eyes and ears, yet they do not see and they do not hear. How is this to be explained? The Israelites, in the course of their long relationship with the Lord in history, beginning with their redemption from Egyptian slavery, had been given ample opportunity to learn

59

the way in which their God acted. They had the opportunity to hear and to see, thereby becoming qualified to testify as the Lord's witnesses. Their *attitude*, however, during the course of this history, showed that they had *not* seen nor heard. Yet in spite of this, *God can use them as witnesses.*

In *verse (43:) 9* Isaiah presents the figure of a great legal process being enacted at the present moment in history—Israel's captivity among the nations. This figure is intended to alert Israel that the present hour in history is the time for a final decision: God or the gods. Is the Lord merely one deity among many deities? Are all the deities of the nations also of divine nature? Or is the Lord the only deity truly divine? Israel must make this final decision now because her relationship with her God is no longer tied to a particular piece of land, and because she is no longer confronted by the nations and their gods who from time to time came against that piece of land. Is the Lord also the God of all nations and of all peoples, irrespective of geographical location? Is the Lord still Israel's God, even among the nations in which she is now scattered? If so, does this negate the supposed divinity of these nations' deities? This is the question on trial.

Verses (43:) 10–13. To spiritually unseeing and unhearing Israel, the Lord declares: "You are my witnesses" (v. 10). This is a public acknowledgment. But how is this possible? Because God *chose* Israel to be His servant (v. 10). He can arouse them from their unseeing and unhearing so that they will "know" and "believe" and "understand" (v. 10). These three verbs refer to one and the same process. They are to know "that it is I" (v. 10). The Lord is the one who is able to create a future out of the ruins of the past. And what they are to know, believe and understand is that He, and He alone, can do this. And this fully

60

personal knowledge will come only from the experience of an encounter with the Living God. It is knowledge that believes, or belief that has knowledge. Thus, when Israel knows that God is truly God—through experience—she may become His witness; she may witness that she has encountered the God who is truly God.

This theme of knowing and believing links this present coming act of salvation—Israel from Babylonian captivity—with God's former, and first, great act of Israel's salvation from Egyptian bondage: "I will also redeem you with an outstretched arm and with judgments. Then I will take you for My people, and I will be your God; and *you shall know* that I am the Lord your God" (Exod 6:6–7). "And when Israel saw the great power which the Lord had used against the Egyptians, the people feared the Lord and *they believed* in the Lord" (Exod 14:31).

It was commonly understood in the myths and polytheistic theologies of the peoples of the Old Testament world (e.g., Sumerians, Assyrians, Babylonians) that the gods had been created. In particular, one Sumerian creation account, called *Enuma Elish,* describes "how the gods had been created," how (gods) Lahmu and Lahamu "came into being," and how (gods) Anshar and Kishar "were created." Thus, the Lord's declaration through His prophet Isaiah is, on one side, a radical and unequivocal denial of these pagan theologies and, on the other, a declaration that Israel's God is the only God: "Before Me there was no god formed, and there will be none after Me" (v. 10). It is now the time for Israel to know this, and to believe this, and thus to *live* in a manner that demonstrates this knowledge and belief. It is now time for Israel to decisively stop vacillating between God and the no-gods of the nations. Prophet Elijah's question of long before was to be finally settled:

61

"How long will you vacillate between two opinions? If the Lord is God, follow Him; but if Baal, follow him" (1 Kgs 18:21).

Israel has had ample encounter with God to know that He is unique, and there is no other like Him. God's uniqueness is not based on theory, but on Israel's actual experience. God has proved Himself to be the only Savior—no other god has ever saved it's people from bondage. And if in the future anyone can help Israel, it can only be He. Therefore, God can say: "I, even I, am the Lord; and there is no savior besides Me" (v. 11).

Four times in this passage God expresses His eternal sameness—three of them intended to remind Israel of His long ago proclamation and salvation through Moses: "I am He" (v. 10); "I, even I, am the Lord" (v. 11); "I am God" (v. 12) (cf. Exod 3:14; 4:11, 12; 6:6, 8). To this great proclamation and resulting action the Israelites, in their present Babylonian captivity, are to be "witnesses" (v. 12). In the fourth instance God declares, "Even from today [and onwards] I am God" (v. 13). There is no discontinuity: "I am God from old, and today I am the same."

And Israel, destroyed and dispersed as she now is, can trust in this: *she remains in God's hand.* The political powers that dominate her world cannot break the bond between Israel and her God. The Lord will act on Israel's behalf, and no one can turn Him back (v. 13).

Do we Christians of the twenty-first century A.D., as the people of the Living God, truly and deeply believe that the deities of the nations in the midst of which we dwell, are no gods, and that the Living Lord is the One and only true God? Do we witness to this by the manner in which we live, both positively and negatively?

43:14-21. The Fall of Babylon and a New Exodus

Verses (43:) 14–15. This passage opens with a description of the living God: "your Redeemer, the Holy One of Israel" (v. 14). "Your Redeemer" is explained in what follows. God has intervened in history on Israel's behalf: "For your sake I have sent to Babylon." This is a reference to Persian Cyrus's capture of Babylon, the coming result of which will be the freedom of the Jews to return to Judah. Here God's sovereignty over worldwide events is evident. It is He who sets up kings and brings them down—in this case the fall of the Babylonian Empire and the rise of the Persian Empire. And all this for the sake of tiny Israel!

Reference is made to the Babylonians becoming "fugitives" (v. 14), that is, those who flee away with no place to go. These are the citizen-residents of the city of Babylon who flee before the advancing armies of Cyrus. One class of residents, the "Chaldeans," is singled out for special reference. They will be driven "into the ships of their rejoicing" (v. 14). Ships were the Chaldeans' pride and joy. From ancient sources we learn that the Chaldeans engaged in the freight shipping trade with Babylon, situated on the Euphrates River, one of their prime ports of trade. They navigated not only the Euphrates River but the Persian Gulf as well. They also used ships built by the Phoenicians for warlike purposes. Many had settled in Babylon from days of antiquity.

Verses (43:) 16–17. God's present act for the sake of Israel is paralleled by His earlier act, which initiated Israel's history: the deliverance at the Red Sea. For the band of fugitives from Egypt, God created "a way through the sea" (v. 16); He also destroyed the Egyptian troops who pursued (note the terms:

Isaiah 43

"chariot," "horse," "army," "mighty man," v. 17). Here Isaiah takes up the basic tradition of Israel's faith onwards through the whole of the Old Testament. The Exodus is frequently celebrated in the Psalms as God's foundation act in creating Israel as His people. For example, Psalm 78:

> He wrought wonders before their fathers,
> In the land of Egypt, in the field of Zoan.
> He divided the sea, and caused them to pass through;
> And He made the waters stand up like a heap (vv. 12–13).
>
> He brought forth streams also from the rock,
> And caused waters to run down like rivers (v. 16).
>
> He led forth His own people like sheep,
> And guided them in the wilderness like a flock;
> And He led them safely, so that they did not fear;
> But the sea engulfed their enemies (vv. 52-53).

Or Psalm 105:

> He sent Moses His servant,
> And Aaron whom He had chosen.
> They performed His wondrous acts among them [i.e., Egypt],
> And miracles in the land of Ham (vv. 25-26).
> Then He brought them out with silver and gold;
> And among His tribes there was not one who stumbled.
> Egypt was glad when they departed;
> for the dread of them had fallen upon them (vv. 37-38).
> He opened the rock, and water flowed out;
> It ran in the dry places like a river (v. 41).
> And He brought forth His people with joy,
> His chosen ones with a joyful shout (v. 43).

Verse (43:) 18. Yet in appears that this very thing, God's initial act of deliverance, "the former things," "the things of the past," are to be forgotten (v. 18), so tremendous and overwhelming is the "new thing" which God is about to do. *This*

64

new thing, as was the old, is the preparation of a way. In the old it was "a way through the sea" (v. 16); in the new it will be "a way in the wilderness" (v. 19). Thus, the new coming Exodus corresponds to the first Exodus.

But does Isaiah really mean that the new will so overshadow the old as to cause the old to be forgotten? More than any other prophet, Isaiah emphatically reminds Israel of God's mighty acts in the past. It would be strange if here he were saying, "Forget what God has done in former days, and consider it no more." What he wants the people to hear is rather, "Stop mournfully looking back and clinging to the past. Open your minds to a new and miraculous act of God lying just ahead of you." The "new thing" which God is about to do is the new thing that Israel had ceased to expect, hope for, or believe in: *a saving act of deliverance from Babylonian bondage.* She thought that God's saving acts were only in the past.

The correspondence between the new thing and the old, the Exodus from Babylonian exile and that from Egypt, consists in two things. First, the same God of the first Exodus becomes the Deliverer and Liberator of His chosen people now in the second Exodus. Here is consistency. The same God who appeared unto Father Abraham many centuries before and led him forth from one land (Chaldea) to another (Canaan) (Gen 12:1-6), later appeared to Moses and said, "I am the God of your father, the God of Abraham" (Exod 3:6). And through Moses God declared to "the elders of Israel" in Egypt, "I will bring you up out of the affliction of Egypt to the land of the Canaanite" (Exod 3:17), now He declares to His chosen and beloved people in modern Babylon (old Chaldea) that He will bring them out from Babylon to the same land to which He had long before safely brought Father Abraham.

Verses (43:) 19–20. Second, this new proclamation of deliverance becomes historical reality by means of a new journey through "the wilderness" (vv. 19, 20). In the course of this journey, this wilderness is to be miraculously transformed. For God gives "water in the wilderness" (v. 20). And the benefits of this miracle of divine grace reach even to the wild creatures living in the desert. The "jackals and the ostriches," both desert animals, will "glorify Me," says the Lord (v. 20). Their joyful cries will be an unconscious praise of the Lord.

Verse (43:) 21. But, is this new act of God, this new Exodus a final act, an end in itself? Not at all. God is to go on dealing with His chosen people, with the people whom He says, "I formed for Myself" (v. 21). This new act of God, this new Exodus, is to be echoed in the praises of the redeemed: they "will declare My praises" (v. 21). Praise telling of God's act has no meaning unless history goes on. There are those of the next generations who will need to be told of God's miraculous act(s) of the past—so that they, too, will know that the Living God of the past is the same today and tomorrow, so that they will know that

> The lovingkindness of the Lord is from everlasting to everlasting on those who fear Him,
> And His righteousness to children's children,
> To those who keep His covenant,
> And who remember His precepts to do them (Ps 103:17).

43:22–28. Israel's Sin and the Lord's Forgiveness

Though not explicitly stated, there appears to lie behind the framework of this passage a charge brought *against the Lord by Israel,* seen perhaps in verse 28, rephrased in the voice of Israel:

"You have delivered Jacob to utter destruction and Israel to shame." Added to this is the exiles' possible protest, implied in the Lord's admonishment in vv. 22-24: "How could You do this, when we have faithfully served You through the worship of sacrifices?" This has put the Lord in the position of defendant, with Israel as His accuser.

This passage, then, is in the form of a trial, but different than the previous trial passages (Isa 41:1–5; 41:21–29; 43:8–13). Here the Lord opposes Israel, His chosen people. He charges them with "sins" and "iniquities" (v. 25), and challenges them to prove Him wrong in court (v. 26). Israel remains silent since the historical evidence supports the Lord's charge (v. 27). Therefore, the Lord has been justified in letting judgment come upon Israel (v. 28). But judgment is for a time only. Out of the very nature of God comes forgiveness (v. 25). And *this* is the focus of the passage!

Verses (43:) 22–24 contain the Lord's response to Israel's implied claim to having served Him faithfully through her sacrifices and offerings. And while there had been those throughout Israel's history who had offered genuine, real and effective worship which God accepted, God's verdict on Israel's worship practice as a whole is that her speech and acts of worship never in actual fact reached Him.

The Hebrew sentence constructions of verses 22–24 have placed the pronoun "Me" in a position of emphasis, to imply the following:

> Not upon *Me* did you call, O Jacob, not for *Me* did you weary yourselves, O Israel.
>
> Not to *Me* did you bring your sheep for burnt offerings, not *Me* did you honor with your sacrifices.
>
> Not for *Me* did you buy fragrant plants with money, not on *Me* did you lavish the fat of your sacrifices.

No, Israel had wearied herself calling upon *other gods,* all the while deluding herself into believing that her intermixed ritual sacrifice to the Lord would make her worship acceptable. In the final days of Judah's existence, Jeremiah spoke of "the sun and the moon and all the stars of the heavens, which they have loved and served and which they have followed and consulted and worshiped" (Jer 8:2). "O Israel," the Lord is saying, "you never truly worshiped Me with your many prayers and sacrifices and offerings. You never truly served Me in the midst of all your ritual fanfare. Rather, you acted as though I were your servant; you wearied Me by making me bear the outrage of your pious sacrifices at the same time I had to tolerate your many sins and iniquities" (v. 24).

In verse 23 the Lord says:

> I have not burdened you with [demands for grain] offerings,
> Nor wearied you with [demands for] incense.

But did not the Lord indeed require sacrifice and incense from Israel as part of her worship? Yes, but only one of the sacrifices was intended to be offered on the occasions of having sinned. All the rest were to be offered within the context of a life lived out ethically and morally before the Lord and with one's neighbor. They were to be visible expressions of such an ethical and moral life. And this is what so wearied the Lord. The offerings were false expressions of lives in ethical and moral decay.

Micah, a prophet contemporary with Isaiah, depicted the ongoing ethical and moral situation of Israel with a question and answer:

> With what shall I come to the Lord
> And bow myself before the exalted God on high?
> Shall I come to Him with burnt offerings,

68

> With yearling calves?
> Does the Lord take delight in thousands of rams,
> In ten thousand rivers of oil? . . .
> He has told you, O man, what is good.
> And what does the Lord require of you?
> But to do justice, to love kindness,
> And to walk humbly with your God? (Mic 6:6–8).

But in spite of the many rams, calves and rivers of oil, Israel's behavior is anything but just and merciful and humble. Micah points to the corrupt business practices in the cities of Israel: ill-gotten treasures, short measures, dishonest scales, false weights, liars and deceitful tongues (Mic 6:10–12).

Jeremiah, in prophesying the coming destruction of Jerusalem and exile, preached to the people of Judah as they came to the Temple to worship. He urged them to reform their ways and actions, to deal justly with each other, and to stop oppressing the helpless. He spoke of their stealing, murder, adultery and perjury in court. He spoke of their burning incense to Baal and other gods, then coming to stand before the Lord in the Temple (Jer 7:2–10). He then declares the Lord's response to all this: "Go ahead, add your burnt offerings to your other sacrifices . . . . For when I brought your forefathers out of Egypt and spoke to them, I did not just give them commands about burnt offerings and sacrifices, but I gave them this command: Obey me, and I will be your God and you will be my people. Walk in all the ways I command you . . . but they did not listen . . . instead, they followed the stubborn inclinations of their evil hearts . . . . From the time your forefathers left Egypt until now . . . I sent you my servants the prophets. But they did not listen to me or pay attention" (NIV, Jer 7:21–26).

Verses (43:) 25–28. We return to the courtroom where God is defending Himself against the accusation of Israel. The

69

facts of history are irrefutable. Israel cannot prove herself righteous before God. She *has* sinned against the Lord, and for so long that the Lord is weary and can bear it no longer. The Lord's verdict is: "So I delivered Jacob to utter destruction, and Israel to scorn" (NIV, v. 28).

But is this the final verdict? No, indeed. For right at the center of this passage, in stark contrast to what precedes and follows, is the proclamation of forgiveness: "I, even I, am the one who wipes out your transgressions—for My own sake—and I will not remember you sins" (v. 25).

This blotting out of sin is in no way merited by Israel, or by you or me. It is a sovereign act of God, rooted in His mercy and compassion *(see* Ps 51:1*)*.

FEAR NOT! I HAVE CHOSEN YOU
(ISAIAH 44)

There are four major units in chapter 44:

- ❑ The Lord, Israel's Creator (vv. 1–5).
- ❑ The Lord, Israel's Rock (vv. 6–8).
- ❑ A Satire on the Foolishness of Idolatry (vv. 9–20).
- ❑ The Lord, Israel's Redeemer (vv. 21–28).

44:1–5. The Lord, Israel's Creator

Verses (44:) 1–2. "But now" (v. 1) closely links this section with the message at the end of chapter 43—Yes, I did deliver you, Jacob, to destruction and scorn when I exiled you to Babylon. *But,* this is what I am *now* saying to you for the future, "Fear not" (v. 2). (We have noted a similar transition linking chapters 42 and 43.)

God addresses Jacob/Israel as His "servant" and His "chosen" one (v. 1). These two designations complement each other: "chosen" expresses God's gracious will in electing Israel from among all the nations; "servant" speaks of the purpose for which Israel has been elected. That purpose is for the "praise" (Isa 43:21) and "glory" (Isa 43:7) of the Master. In the earlier reference (Isa 43:7), God uses three different creation story terms found in Genesis 1: "created" (*bara'*), "formed" (*yatsar*) and "made" (*'asah*). In the present 44:2 reference, He uses two of these terms: "made" (*'asah*) and "formed" (*yatsar*). The Lord, then, sets Himself in relation to Israel as her Creator, just as He has in Isaiah 43:1. But He is not only Israel's Creator, He is also her "Helper" (v. 2). Therefore, Israel is to "fear not" (v. 2).

In Isaiah 43:2 Israel was to put aside fear because of a *past* action of God on her behalf: "I have redeemed you," a reference to the first Exodus when God rescued Israel from Egyptian bondage. But in Isaiah 44:2, Israel is to put aside fear because of a *future* action of God on her behalf.

Verse (44:) 3. This future action of God is taken up in verse 3. God will pour out an abundance of "water" upon the "thirsty [one]." This thirsty one is Israel in her present dried up and parched spiritual condition. God's spiritually life-giving water will not be a mere passing shower, but like the "streams on the dry ground" in the rainy season.

But this great outpouring will not be upon the present generation of exiled Jews, even when they reach the homeland in Judah, but upon the generations to come. The poured out water will be in the form of God's "Spirit" and His "blessing" upon the present generation's "offspring" and "descendents." Because of this great outpouring of God's Spirit and blessing, Israel will experience abundant increase. This increase will come by two means: biological growth (v. 4) and conversion growth (v. 5).

Verse (44:) 4. For the *biological growth*, the metaphor of trees growing beside streams of water is used: "They will spring up. . . like poplars by streams of water" (v. 4). The tree translated here as "poplars" (Heb., *'arabim*) grows from six to eight meters in height and thrives best along the sides of rivers and brooks. It grows very quickly and is easily multiplied by cutting off small branches. When these cuttings are pushed into moist soil, they grow roots almost immediately and spring up rapidly. Thus the Lord uses these willows as a metaphor for the rapidity with which the future generations of Israel will increase. To speak of Israel's rapid biological growth as a direct result of God's "blessing" is no mere accident of words. As God has used creation language in verse 2, so He continues to do so here. We read in Genesis 1:28, "And God *blessed* them [the first male and female humans], and said to them, 'Be fruitful and multiply'." So God is speaking here of a re-creation of His people.

The prophet Ezekiel also joins the metaphor of "water" with God's "Spirit" (Ezek 36:25–29) in reference to the future generations of God's people. Here the primary implication is spiritual cleansing and a spiritual enabling to walk in the Lord's statutes. But an increase in the number of people is also promised: "I will increase their men like a flock . . . so will the waste cities be filled with flocks of men." And with this spiritual cleansing and refilling of the cities of Judah will come spiritual knowledge: "Then they will know that I am the Lord" (Ezek 36:37–38). The future generations of God's people, because of God's Spirit within them, will have new wisdom: there is no god except the Lord! Thus, perhaps Isaiah, in Isaiah 44:3–4, is comparing the willows by the streams of water with Spirit-filled people who make quick progress in attaining spiritual wisdom.

Verse (44:) 5 speaks of *conversion growth*. The future generations of Israel will also increase by the addition of proselytes—as people of other nations and other faiths turn to Israel and to her God. *Foreigners* will join the community of Israel and declare themselves to be worshippers of the Lord. "This one *will say* . . . . That one *will call [himself]* . . . . Another will *write* on his hand"—all three verbs express faith in the God of Israel on the basis of *personal* decision. This implies the new convert's desire to give some form of public expression to his conversion: some adopt a new name—Jacob or Israel; some will write on their hands "Belonging to the Lord" (there was some practice in the biblical world of a slave cutting his master's name on his hand); some will simply declare with the mouth, "I am the Lord's."[1] All of these declarations are marks of ownership. Further to be noted is that when these non-Israelites turned to Israel's God, they also joined the community of Israel. "One could only confess the God of Israel as his lord if he took his place among the people who served this God."[2]

In other words, Israel's faith could never be divorced from the great acts of deliverance and salvation that God wrought on her behalf. And any who joined Israel by confession of faith could justly say, "We were slaves to Pharaoh in Egypt; and the Lord brought us from Egypt with a mighty hand" (Deut 6:21); or

> When the Lord brought back the captive ones of Zion,
> We were like those who dream.
> Then our mouth was filled with laughter,
> And our tongue with joyful shouting (Ps 126:1–2)

This is so with those today who profess faith in the Living God. We do so by justly claiming participation in the great act of deliverance and salvation wrought by Jesus Christ on the Cross 2,000 years ago. "In Him we have redemption through His blood, the forgiveness of our trespasses, according to the riches of His grace" (Eph 1:7). All who by faith become God's children "are of God's household" (Eph 2:19).

---

[1] Claus Westermann, *Isaiah 40-66, A Commentary* (Philadelphia: Westminster 1969) p. 137.

[2] Westermann, *Isaiah 40-66*, pp. 137–128.

44:6-8. The Lord, Israel's Rock

Again, in a trial speech the Lord confronts the gods of the nations (see also Isa 41:1–5; 41:21–28; and 43:8–15). The "case" here is similar to that in the previous three: that only the Lord is God. And, as in the others, this proof is found in history: there has always been a direct correlation between the Lord's speech and action. And, as in the third trial speech (Isa 43:8–15), the Lord calls Israel to be His witnesses.

Verse (44:) 6. "Thus says the Lord!" (v. 6) Who is this "Lord?" He identifies Himself by three titles.

First, the Lord is "King of Israel" (also in Isa 41:21; 43:15). We first encounter the Lord's claim to kingship over Israel in 1 Samuel 8:7, where the Lord recognizes His people's rejection of Him as their king. From a human viewpoint, it appeared that the Lord had relinquished His kingship. "But now, O Israel," says the Lord, "you have a King. I never abandoned the throne of Israel. You are still my subjects. And as King I come now to act on your behalf."

Second, the Lord is Israel's "Redeemer." This title defines the King's action on Israel's behalf. In this title, the Lord reminds Israel that He is her kinsman-protector, who will save Israel (see comments on Isa 41:14).

Third, God is "Lord of hosts." This title for God occurs 279 times in the Old Testament. Of these, 60 are in Isaiah alone. Though Isaiah has used the title many times in the first segment of the book (chap. 1–39), this is the first occurrence in this second segment (chap. 40–55). This title defines the Lord as more than merely the God of Israel. He is the all-powerful sovereign and controller of *all* human and superhuman forces. With His unseen armies the Lord will bring about His people's redemption. We are given a glimpse of the Lord's unseen "hosts" in 2 Kings 6:8–19. Elisha and his servant were living in the northern Israelite town of Dothan. One night, they were surrounded by "horses and chariots, and a great [Syrian] army" (v. 14). When he observed their situation, the servant cried out, "Alas, my master! What shall we do?" (v. 15). Elisha suggests to his frightened servant that he need not fear because "those who are with us are more than those who are with them" (v. 16). Elisha then prays for the Lord to "open his [spiritual] eyes that he may see" (v. 17). The Lord does so, and the servant sees "the mountain full of horses and chariots of fire all around" (v. 17). These horses and chariots were part of the unseen heavenly forces that the Lord, the King of Israel, commands.

Verse (44:) 7. The Lord asks the nations and their gods, "Since the time I founded the ancient people (Heb., *'am 'olam*), who preaches (Heb., *yiqra'*) as I do?" *Yiqra'* refers to the continued preaching of prophecy. Thus, the Lord shows Himself as the God of prophecy since the time that He founded the "ancient people." In Isaiah 42:5, *'am* "people" signifies the human race. In Job 22:15 *'olam* is the time of the old world before the flood. Thus, here in Isaiah 44:7, the reference to the prophetic preaching of the Lord reaches back even to the history of mankind in the Garden of Eden.

The challenge to the nations is: Is there any nation's god who has preached prophecy like I have? Is there any nation's god who has guided its history by proclamations whose fulfillments have been visible and known, thus enabling that nation to know that this god can be relied on to guide them in the present and future? This challenge is not merely hypothetical. It is a real challenge among real nations whose peoples were indoctrinated with just such claims about the pagan deities. For example, in the ancient Babylonian story of creation, entitled *When on High,* the gods are made to say:

> Thou, Marduk, art the most honored of the great gods. . . .
> From this day unchangeable shall be thy pronouncement.
> To raise or bring low—these shall be in thy hand.
> Thy utterance shall be true, thy command shall be unimpeachable.[3]

A similar claim is made in a *Hymn to Shamash,* the Babylonian sun-god:

> Shamash whose promise no god makes vain,
> Whose command is not turned back.[4]

The Jewish exiles in Babylon had been surrounded for years by such pagan religious influences. *They* needed to see and know that there is a significant difference between the Lord of hosts and the multitude of other so-called gods. They needed to be reminded of what Judean King Hezekiah knew and prayed in 701 BC when the Syrian armies were at the gates of Jerusalem:

> O Lord of hosts, God of Israel . . . . You are God, You alone, of all the kingdoms of the earth . . . Sennacherib . . . has sent to reproach the living God. Truly, Lord, the kings of Assyria have laid waste all the nations and their lands, and have cast their gods into the fire; *for they were not gods, but the work of men's hands*—wood and stone. Therefore they destroyed them. Now therefore, O Lord our God, save us from his hand, that all the kingdoms of the earth may know that You are the Lord, you alone (NIV, Isa 37:16–20).

Verse (44:) 8. The Lord turns to the Exiles in direct address: "Do not be afraid." Indeed, nearly two centuries after

---

[3] James B. Pritchard, *Ancient Near Eastern Texts* (Princeton: Princeton University Press, 1955, Second ed.) p. 66.

[4] Cited by Westermann, *Isaiah 40-66,* p. 141, footnote a.

King Hezekiah's affirmation of trust in the Lord, these discouraged and fearful Exiles need have no fear of the great catastrophe coming upon the nations, brought by Cyrus and his armies. In the midst of this world upheaval one nation after another would be overthrown. Their gods would be shown to be helpless and worthless. But Israel need not fear: "Have I not long since announced it to you and declared it?" says the Lord (v. 8).

In light of this, The Lord declares Himself to be a "Rock" to His people (v. 8). Twenty-one times in the confessions of confidence in the Psalms God is called "Rock."[5] This figure implies true security and trustworthiness. Thus for God's people, the words "there is no God beside Me" mean that "He alone has proved to be our Refuge"—He, and no other person or thing!

44.9–20. A Satire on the Foolishness of Idolatry

This passage is in the form of a taunt-song. It is the longest satire on idolatry in the Old Testament and stands in stark contrast with the unique claims for the Lord in verses 6–8.

Isaiah uses sarcasm to make his point. And the target of his sarcasm is not the great state gods of Babylonian national religion, such as Bel and Nebo (which *are* the target of his sarcasm in Isaiah 46). Rather, the target is the homemade, domestic idolatry of every day life.

This taunt-song divides into two parts. The first, verses 9–11, is a general verdict passed on the makers and

---

[5] Psalm 18:2 (2 times), 31, 46; 19:14; 28:1; 31:2, 3; 42:9; 61:2 (2 times), 6, 7; 71:3 (2 times); 78:35; 89:26; 92:15; 94:22; 95:1; 144:1.

worshippers of idols: they are to "be put to shame." The second, verses 12–20 describe the process of idol making.

Verses (44:) 9–11. The song opens with a very strong condemnation of the *makers* of idols: "All who make idols are nothing." The Hebrew word for "nothing" (*tohu*) here is the same as used for "void" or "empty" at the beginning of creation (Gen 1:1). The *worshippers* ("witnesses," v. 9) of these idols "see" nothing and "know" nothing. Both of these verbs have here the sense of "experience"—the worshippers have no experience of anything done by these gods of "no profit," made by "mere men" (v. 11).

Verses (44:) 12–20 describe the process of the manufacture of idols—but in reverse order! With the "nothingness" of idols in mind, Isaiah describes the way idols come into being by describing the operation in reverse back to its initial stage. The carpenter "shapes wood" (v. 13); but he first "cuts cedars" (v. 14); and before that he "plants a fir" (v. 14)—all a product of man's labor! Or so it seems. Yet the ultimate existence or non-existence of these idols depends upon whether or not it rains, for "the rain makes it grow" (v. 14).

The origin of household or local shrine idols, then, can be traced and known. How different from the God of Israel, whose "origin" cannot be known, and of whom there can be no images made. The Old Testament writers never speculate on the origin of God. For them it is simply an assumption of faith that God had no beginning and was before all creation:

> Before the mountains were born,
> Or You gave birth to the earth and the world,
> From everlasting to everlasting, You are God (Ps 90:2).

> The heavens are Yours, the earth also is Yours;
> The world and all it contains,

You have founded them (Ps 89:11)

> For great is the Lord, and greatly to be praised;
> He is to be feared above all gods.
> For all the gods of the peoples are idols,
> But the Lord made the heavens.
> Splendor and majesty are before Him,
> Strength and beauty are in His sanctuary (Ps 96:4–6).

Verse 13 is very pointed satire: the idol is made into the "form of a man," with the "beauty of man." And for what purpose? Merely to "sit in a house"! How absolutely opposite this is from the Living God of Israel who said,

> Heaven is My throne, and the earth is My footstool.
> Where then is a house you could build for me? (Isa 66:1).

One may well ask, what kind of gods are these that must dwell in houses, whose makers

> Fasten [them] with nails and with hammers
> So that [they] will not totter,

and

> They must be carried,
> Because they cannot walk ? (Jer 10:4–5).

The ultimate irony here is that the idol is a statue of a man, made in the image of a man, but lifeless, standing in a shrine, while all the time the true image of God, the living man, is walking around outside! How absurd that the image of God should bow to the image of man, which is nothing but "a block of wood" (v. 19).

Verses 15–19 give a satirical contrast between the two uses to which the idol worshipper puts the wood cut from the forest. With half he makes a fire, roasts his meat, eats and warms himself. With the other half he makes an idol, falls before it, worships it and prays to it. And the maker-worshipper fails to see the foolish incongruity of his two utterances: "Ah, I am warm, I have seen the fire," and "Deliver me, for you are my god" (vv. 16–17). Warmth for his body, and heat for cooking his food, is the extent of the help the idol worshipper may expect from his so-called god.

A non-biblical anecdote concerning the ancient Greek god-hero Hercules illustrates the "usefulness" of idols. The so-called god Hercules is said to have possessed enormous strength, and thus performed "twelve labors" on behalf of Eurytheus king of Mycenae. It is said that a certain Diagoras, pupil of the fifth century B.C. Greek philosopher Democritus, once threw a wooden idol of Hercules into the fire, saying humorously, "Come now, Hercules, perform your thirteenth labor, and help me cook the turnips."[6] So irrational is idolatry.

A literal translation of verse 18, gives an apt description of those who make and worship idols: "They know nothing and they understand nothing, for smeared over are their eyes [preventing them] from seeing and their hearts [preventing them] from comprehending." The implication here most likely is that the worshipper is responsible for the smearing of his own eyes. Psalm 115:4–8 is another short satire on the foolishness of idol worship, ending with the observation:

> Those who make them [i.e., idols] will become like them,
> Everyone who trusts in them (Ps 115:8).

The reference in Isaiah 44:18 to the "smeared over" eyes of the maker-worshipper of idols, may be a likening to the eyes of the idol which he worships. In some cases, the eyes of the idols

---

[6] C. F. Keil and F. Delitzsch, *Isaiah: Commentary on the OT, vol. 7* (Grand Rapids: Eerdmans, reprint, 1986) p. 211.

were smeared with white paint—eyes, but not eyes, appearing to see, but not seeing.

The Old Testament recognizes that idolaters are spiritually blinded. This is similar to Paul's view in Romans 1–2. Paul further understands this to be a blindness that is partly willful and partly the work of an outside power. To the Corinthians Paul wrote, "If our gospel is veiled, it is veiled to those who are perishing, in whose case the god of this world has blinded the minds of the unbelieving, that they might not see the light of the gospel of the glory of Christ, who is the image of God" (2 Cor 4:3–4).

44:21–28. The Lord, Israel's Redeemer

Verses (44:) 21–23. "Remember these things!" (v. 21). Here God reminds Israel what He has saved them from—idolatry (vv. 9–20). But also they are to remember the greatness and uniqueness of the Lord—that He is King of Israel, Redeemer, Lord of Hosts and Israel's Rock (vv. 6–8). And again God reminds Israel that "you are My servant," that "I have formed you," and this master-servant relationship assures that "you will not be forgotten by Me" (v. 21).

Redemption is again promised (v. 22). In fact, from God's perspective, redemption is already an accomplished fact— "I *have* wiped out your transgressions . . . and your sins . . . I *have* redeemed you." *This is Gospel in the Old Testament!* In light of this, God extends the invitation: "Return to Me"—to *God*. Isaiah is concerned with a *spiritual* restoration, not just a political restoration to the land of Judah. "God *has* redeemed you, so return to Him now." Such is the jubilation at this redemption that all of "earth" is called to praise God: the "mountains," the "forest," the "lower parts"—the place of the dead. (Even the place of the dead is under God's control; cf. Ps 139:7–9; Amos 9:2.) And redeemed Israel will be the "glory" of God displayed to the world (v. 23). Later, Isaiah will declare:

> You will also be a crown of beauty in the hand of the Lord,
> And a royal diadem in the hand of your God (Isa 62:3).

The crowning achievement of all God's work in history will be His own redeemed people. God was to be seen and known through redeemed Israel in the Old Testament. But this is no less true of the New Testament Church. In Ephesians chapter 1 Paul speaks of those of us who are "in Christ Jesus" (v. 1). We have experienced "redemption through His blood" and "forgiveness of our trespasses" (v. 7). All this is "to the end that we . . . should be to the praise of His glory" (v. 12; also vv. 6, 14). Thus, says Paul, "the manifold wisdom of God" is to "be made known through the church" (Eph 3:10).

How will God accomplish the physical redemption of His people from Babylonian exile? Through "Cyrus, My Shepherd" (v. 28). But it is "the Lord, your Redeemer" (v. 24), who causes all this to happen. "Your Redeemer" picks up the theme of previous chapters (Isa 43:1, 14; 44:6, 22,23). Israel in Babylonian exile would find difficulty in seeing salvation in the advancing Persian troops. But the coming Persian conquest of Babylon is *God's* doing and will provide redemption for his people, Israel.

Verses (44:) 24–26 summarize the verdicts of all the preceding trial speeches (Isa 41:1–5; 41:21–28; 43:8–15; 44:6–8): the Lord is God of creation, Lord of history and of its meaning, He overthrows false diviners, and establishes the word of His own prophets by fulfilling it.

Verse 24 begins with God glorifying Himself as the creator of all things. The emphasis in the Hebrew is upon "I," implying

"I *alone*, the Lord, am maker of all things." This form was often used in the Babylonian texts in self-glorification speeches of the gods. But in these Babylonian texts, the form expresses polytheism, for one god boasts of his greatness and power as compared with the other gods. When used in the speech of the Lord by Isaiah, there are no rival gods:

> I [alone] am the Lord, there is no other;
> Besides Me there is no God (Isa 45:5).

The Lord proves Himself to be the only true God, not by being greater and more powerful than other gods, but by being the one who remains forever:

> I am the first and I am the last,
> And there is no God besides Me (Isa 44:6).

Verse 25 speaks of "boasters," "diviners" and "wise men." During Babylon's final years, king Nabonidus (555–539 B.C.), in the face of the advancing Persian threat, rescued idols from temples across the Babylonian Empire. He brought them to Babylon for safekeeping. With these idols came a great number of priests, prophets and diviners representing a great variety of gods. They all gave predictions about the future of Babylon. But the Lord will not allow any of these to turn Him from His chosen course of action—the restoration and re-inhabitation of Jerusalem. And this will require the overthrow of Babylon!

The climax of the announcement of God's redemption is the mention of Cyrus, the Persian emperor, who is about to enter Babylon. By this time every prophet in Babylon has claimed his god to be responsible for the phenomenal success of Cyrus and his armies. But the Lord claims that Cyrus belongs to Him. Cyrus is the Lord's *Shepherd* (v. 28). "Shepherd" was a customary term in the Old Testament world for a political ruler (see Isa 40:9; 2 Sam 5:2; Jer 23:1–4, Ezek 34:2–24). Usually, "The

Lord's shepherd" could only have been applied to an *Israelite* king. Therefore, this title, when applied to pagan Cyrus, must have been quite a shock to pious Jews. And Isaiah 45:1 makes it seem even worse: Cyrus is God's *anointed!* And Isaiah 45:9 shows the negative reaction of the Jews to such an idea through God's allegorical question, "Will the clay say to the potter, 'What are you doing?'"

Should you, Israel the clay, challenge what I the Potter am doing?

Verses 44:27–28. In summary, this passage declares that the Lord is *God of word and God of act.* God's word and God's act together form a powerful, irresistible combination. What is God's word to the Exiles in Babylon? *Jerusalem will be rebuilt!* The assurance is that, based on God's previous record of fulfilling prophecy, Jerusalem will certainly be rebuilt—*if the Lord says so!* He will act! But how? By Cyrus (v. 28). Cyrus will do exactly what I am planning, and exactly what you, the Exiles, are longing for. You want Jerusalem to be rebuilt? So do I, and Cyrus will accomplish it! Of Cyrus, God says: "He will *perform* [NIV, "fulfill"] all My *desire*" (v. 28).

The words are important here. "Perform" is from the same Hebrew root as is "peace" (*shalem* perform and *shalom* peace). "Peace" describes a relationship or situation of "wholeness" or "completeness." So Cyrus will bring about a state of "peace" in the entire biblical world, and will bring to completion the desire of God—the rebuilding of Jerusalem. The term *hephets* is used often by Isaiah to express the Lord's will and purpose. For example:

> My *purpose* will be established,
> And I will accomplish all My *good pleasure* (*hephets*) (Isa 46:10),

or

85

> So shall my word be which goes forth from My mouth;
> It shall not return to Me empty,
> Without accomplishing what I *desire* (*haphats*) (Isa 55:11).

(See also Isa 48:11; 53:10; 56:4).

Jerusalem is the focus of the Lord's plan. The call of Cyrus and the fall of Babylon prepare for the restoration of Jerusalem, the Lord's City.

THE LORD WILL BE KNOWN (ISAIAH 45)

There are three major units in chapter 45:

- ❑ The Lord Calls Cyrus (vv. 1–8).
- ❑ The Lord Answers Israel's Complaints (vv. 9–13).
- ❑ The Lord's Salvation Is to the Ends of the Earth (vv. 14–25).

45:1–8. The Lord Calls Cyrus

God now speaks to Cyrus directly as His anointed prince (v. 1), whom He has called by name (vv. 3, 4). The Lord declares that He will go before Cyrus in person, breaking down all opposition, and giving him access to wealth hidden in secret vaults (vv. 2-3). The Lord's purpose in acting in such manner is (1) that Cyrus will know that the Lord is God (v. 3), and (2) that all throughout Cyrus's empire will know that the Lord alone is God (v. 6). In sum, that the whole world may know that it is the Lord, God of Israel, who is in charge of everything that happens on earth.

Did Cyrus ever hear of this prophecy? We cannot know, as he makes no mention of it in his own records. If he did, however, he ignored it, for in his records he gives the credit for his success against Babylon to Marduk, Babylon's own chief god—Cyrus claimed that Marduk was using him to punish the last kings of Babylon because of their ruling with oppression, and neglect of Marduk's sanctuary. But Cyrus does not need to know of Isaiah's prophecy, for Isaiah was giving an interpretation of coming historical events from the standpoint of the Lord's sovereignty. The biblical view is that God controls history, in the past and in the present, and that He uses secular human leaders to carry out His plans, whether or not they acknowledge Him. This view is seen in Isaiah's earlier address concerning Assyria (Isa 10:5–11):

> Assyria, the rod of My anger
> And the staff in whose hands is My indignation,
> I send it against a godless nation . . . .
> Yet it does not so intend
> Nor does it plan so in its heart,
> But rather it is its purpose to destroy (Isa 10:5–7).

This view is also seen in Jeremiah's address concerning Babylon: "I [the Lord] will send . . . to Nebuchadnezzar king of Babylon, My servant, and will bring them against this land . . . and I will utterly destroy them" (Jer 25:9; cf. 27:5–7).

Verses (45:) 1–3 contain "coronation" language concerning Cyrus. There are many similarities between the royal coronation language that is common in ancient near eastern texts on the enthronement of a king and what is said here about Cyrus. It is interesting to note Cyrus's own account of his accession to the Babylonian throne, in which he celebrates his defeat of Babylon. He says that Marduk looked "for the upright prince whom he would have to take his hand . . . he called Cyrus . . . he nominated him to be ruler over all . . . [Cyrus] tried to behave with justice and righteousness . . . [Marduk] gave orders that he go against . . . Babylon . . . [Marduk] made him take the road to Babylon and [Marduk] went at his side like a friend and comrade."[1] But what Cyrus

---

[1] T. Fish, "The Cyrus Cylinder," in *Documents from Old Testament Times*, ed. D. Winton Thomas. (London: Thomas Nelson, 1958) p. 92.

credits to a pagan god, Isaiah credits to the Living God of Israel. Isaiah says: Cyrus is the Lord's "anointed" (v. 1), the Lord holds Cyrus "by the right hand" (v. 1), the Lord calls him "by name" (vv. 3, 4), the Lord gives Cyrus a "title of honor" (v. 4), the Lord "girds" Cyrus for action (v. 5).

There are some important terms here. The most astonishing, and, for the Jews, the most shocking, is the Lord's calling Cyrus his *anointed*, His messiah (Heb., *meshiah*). This title is normally applied to Israel's high priest or to Israel's king. It would later become Judaism's term for its expected Deliverer. It refers to one who is anointed with oil; this anointing is a sign of being commissioned by the Lord for a special task. The amazing thing is that a title, always previously applied only to an Israelite—one who mediated the rule or will of the Lord among His people—should now be applied to a foreigner. This means, however, that God may chose whomever He wills to do his bidding. What He once did through Israel's king, he may now do through a foreign king. And as God earlier called the Assyrian to destroy (Isa 10:5–6), so now He calls the Persian to rebuild (Isa 45:13).

Verses (45:) 4–5. In spite of the exalted task that the Lord has entrusted to Cyrus, however, God sets clear limits on his role (vv. 4–5). Cyrus' task is "for the sake of . . . Israel." It is Israel who is God's servant, not Cyrus. "Servant" implies a relationship of intimacy and permanence. Cyrus' relationship with the Lord is neither intimate nor permanent. He is commissioned to one specific task—and this is for Israel's good, not for the glory of himself or his empire. Furthermore, "You have not known Me," God says. The contrast is emphatic and deliberate. The Lord knows Cyrus and is controlling him. But Cyrus will not acknowledge the Lord, he will not be converted, nor be assimilated into the people of God.

Verses (45:) 6–7. But there are no limitations on God! The Lord will be known "from the rising to the setting of the sun" (v. 6). From the geographical standpoint of Israel, the sun rises somewhere far to the east, and sets westward in the Mediterranean Sea. The Persian Empire extended from India in the east to the borders of Greece in the west. The deported and exiled Jews were scattered throughout this entire Persian world, "from the rising to the setting of the sun." God's people, Israel, were called to be His witnesses on this larger world stage. And though there would indeed be a return to Judah and a rebuilding of Jerusalem and the cities of Judah, not all Jews would return. Many would continue to live on in the farthest reaches of the empire, generation after generation—even into this 20th century A.D.!

Verse (45:) 8. But God intends to be known in more than just the Persian Empire. He has the entire world in view, as is made clearer in Isaiah 45:23: "To me every knee will bow, every tongue will swear allegiance."

And herein lies the task of all God's people, everywhere. We are to witness to the "righteousness" of God (v. 8) by making His way the governing principle by which we live. And then, in all God's earth, shall "righteousness spring up" (v. 8).

45:9–13. The Lord Answers Israel's Complaints

Verses (45:) 9–11. Both verses 9 and 10 open with the words "Woe to . . . " In the prophetic literature these words usually precede the pronouncement of doom. In the wisdom literature, however, they condemn an attitude or a habit of action. Isaiah uses the words here as the wisdom teachers do.

He addresses those who were habitually questioning the ways of God in relation to Persian Cyrus (see Isa 44:28–45:4). The question and complaint was: How can the Lord use a pagan foreigner as "shepherd" (Isa 44:28) and "anointed" (Isa 45:1)?

Those who are questioning the ways of God are said to be "quarreling" with God. This is a strong word in the Hebrew, used of legal action—taking someone to court for some wrong they have done. Such "quarrelers" are spoken of in terms of two metaphors. The first is that of the potter's work for the creation of man. The idea of a pot questioning or criticizing what the potter is doing is ridiculous and absurd. The potter has unlimited power over his material. The pot has no right to object either to *what* the potter does or *how* he does it. Likewise, God has the sole right to decide what He does. This point is reinforced by a second, even more absurd metaphor. Imagine an unborn baby questioning or criticizing his father or mother for what they are producing! God then makes the point very clear, as it applies to Him, using both metaphors in reverse order in speaking of "my sons" and "the work of my hands" (v. 11).

Verses (45:) 12–13 expand the imagery of the potter in terms of God's original work of creation. He created the heavens and the stars in them, the earth and humankind upon it (Isa 44:24–26). As creator, God is Lord of His creation; He commands the host of the stars (Isa 40:26). This is the basis for His lordship over the ongoing events of history. This lordship is brought to focus on one particular point, the rousing up of Cyrus to set Israel free. The point being made is that God is about to do a new "creation," and *He has the sole right to do so and to do so in a manner He so chooses*: He *will* free the Jewish exiles and He *will* rebuild Jerusalem and He *will* use Cyrus to do so. The people may object, but this is what God is going to do! (see Isa 44:28).

All this is to be done without "any payment [NIV, bribe] or reward" (v. 13). This may have either of two meanings: (1) Cyrus is to derive no profit from performing this work of setting God's people free and rebuilding God's city; the only reason for this dual action is the will of God; or (2) no price will be required from either God's people or from the city of Jerusalem; Persian Cyrus will pay all—because this is the will of God.

45:14–25. The Lord's Salvation Is to the Ends of the Earth

These verses look beyond Israel's immediate future into a time far in the future—perhaps messianic or end times. But they do so in terms drawn from Israel's historical context of exile and restoration.

Verses (45:) 14–17 picture a great historical *reversal*. Those peoples who had once been enemies and oppressors of Israel: (1) will voluntarily come and bring tribute to God's people—"the products of Egypt and the merchandise of Cush;" (2) they will recognize that Israel's God is active in history—"Surely, God is with you"; and (3) they will acknowledge the reality and uniqueness of Israel's God—"there is none else, no other God" (v. 14). The "Sabeans" are specifically mentioned (see Isa 43:3). These were inhabitants of the Nile Valley in Egypt. The picture of them coming "in chains" probably does not refer to actual captivity, but to voluntary putting on of chains as a symbol of submission.

Verse 14 pictures a tradition found elsewhere in the Old Testament, that one day all peoples of the earth would join in pilgrimage to Zion, bringing lavish gifts, and acknowledging the Lord as the true God (see Isa 2:2–4; 60:1-14; 66:18-24; Zech 14:16; Ps 87).

The words of verse 15 appear to be Isaiah's own observation that God is hidden and unknowable, except as He deliberately chooses to make Himself known.

Verse (45:) 18. And God has chosen to make Himself known—through His creation. God created the world in an orderly fashion, not just as a chaos (see Gen 1), in order that it could be "inhabited" by the whole of mankind. God is the Creator God of the whole world and all its inhabitants. This gives validity to God's right to use any nation or person—in this specific instance, Cyrus—to serve His purpose. This also gives validity to God's concern for the salvation of all mankind (in the verses that follow).

Verse (45:) 19. The references to "secret", "dark" and "waste" places perhaps all refer to the futile magic arts of the occult and their false gods. God is saying that He does not speak in such things, but through His clear revelation to Israel. This verse is important in a biblical doctrine of revelation. We are assured that God does not make Himself obscure in such a way that mankind must seek Him through superstition or the occult. On the contrary, His revelation is clear and unambiguous, and is the only source of moral guidance: "I, the Lord, speak righteousness [NIV, truth], declaring things that are upright."

Verses (45:) 20–25. Here we find one of the high points of the Old Testament evangelistic message: *God's call to salvation is universal.*

The call goes out to the "fugitives of the nations" (v. 20). In the immediate historical context of Cyrus's advance, these "fugitives" would be the defeated Babylonians, who, when fleeing before Cyrus, carried their "wooden idols" with them, hoping to find help from such gods. But, says Isaiah, they "pray to a god that cannot save." Such idolatrous persons have "no knowledge" (v. 20). This seems to imply that idolaters act in ignorance, not merely in willful rebellion.

The call to the defeated idolaters is repeated in verse 22, but now it is unmistakably universal: "all the ends of the earth" are invited to come and enter into *God's* salvation, "for *I* am God, and there is no other" who can save. This Old Testament view is reaffirmed by Peter's Holy Spirit inspired declaration concerning Jesus the Son of God: "There is salvation in no one else; for there is no other name under heaven that has been given among men, by which we must be saved" (Acts 4:12).

The goal of all God's work on the stage of world history is the confession by each *individual* of His total Lordship: "Every knee will bow, every tongue will swear allegiance." Here is the Old Testament's preview of the New Testament's call to personal acceptance of God's salvation and submission to the Lordship of the Living God. Paul quotes this verse twice in the New Testament, in Romans 14:11 in reference to the final judgment, and in Philippians 2:10–11, referring to the exaltation of Jesus Christ. In the latter reference, Paul takes a text originally referring to the Creator God Himself and applies it directly to Jesus!

This passage (Isa 45:20–25) looks forward to a new, non-ethnic, non-political concept of the future people of God, gathered from all the ends of the earth.

THE LORD WHO CARRIES YOU
(ISAIAH 46)

There are three major units in Chapter 46:

- ☐ Who Carries Whom? (vv. 1–4).
- ☐ Who is Like the Lord? (vv. 5–7).
- ☐ Remember the Past; Look to the Future (vv. 8–13).

Two major contrasts are contained in this chapter. One is between lifeless idols that must be carried and supported and the Living Lord who carries and supports His people. The other is between the Lord's proposal to have Cyrus rebuild Jerusalem and exiled Israel's refusal to approve His plan.

46:1–4. Who Carries Whom?

Verses (46:) 1–2. Bel and Nebo, two prominent state gods of Babylon are mentioned (v. 1). In the Babylonian mythology, Bel was originally the god of heaven and father of the gods. His name appears as part of other names such as Bel-shazzar. Later, he became merged with Marduk, the patron god of the city of Babylon. He is sometimes called Bel-Marduk.

Nebo was thought to be the son of Marduk, and was the patron god of the Babylonian kings. His name often appears (with variation of spelling) in names such as Nebu-chadnezzar or Nabo-polassar.

Both Bel and Nebo were also depicted in idol form in Babylonian temples. The scene in verse 1 is that the worshippers of these gods try to carry off their statues to safety. The sight of these great idols, loaded in horizontal position on various "beasts and cattle," being transported just like the other fleeing refugees before the approaching Cyrus, brings forth a bit of satire from Isaiah. Bel and Nebo, like their images, are "bowed down and stooped over," supposedly watching over the parapet of the heavens as their own images are carted off—and they are powerless to stop such indignity! The irony of it all is that the worshippers of Bel and Nebo must save their gods, for the gods cannot even save themselves. Instead of the gods bearing their people in a time of calamity, they themselves must be borne and become a great "burden" (v. 2).

Verses (46:) 3–4. A tremendous contrast is seen in verses 3–4. Israel is called to notice this contrast. Instead of carrying idols, Israel has been carried by the Lord "from before being born . . . from the womb" (v. 3), that is, from before they were even a people called out of Egypt. Now Israel is in "old age," with "grey hairs" (v. 4), and the Lord, in His mercy, is still carrying them. He plans to go right on doing so. Here is an echo of Moses' reminder to Israel just before crossing into Canaan long years before: "in the wilderness . . . the Lord your God carried you, just as a man carries his son, in all the way which you have walked" (Deut 1:31).

Here is the biblical view of the oneness of the Living Lord: He is unchangeable, the same yesterday, today and tomorrow. Thus, the Lord proves His deity precisely at the point where other gods fail: the ability to carry His people through disaster and national collapse. Of significance here is that the Hebrew word for "bear" (v. 4) is the same as in Isaiah 53:4 and 11. God who bears His people is also the Servant who bears His people's "sicknesses" (Isa 53:4) and "iniquities" (Isa 53:11).

46:5–7. Who Is Like the Lord?

The temptation of exiled Israel was to compare God with the gods of Babylon, to view Him as just another of the deities. "How absurd!" says God. How can you compare me to a made-to-order god? Indeed, how absurd is the idea that a man can order a god at the goldsmith's, just because materials are available (v. 6). How absurd to compare the Living Lord with a god who is unable to move, who must be represented by an image, an image that must be carried about on men's shoulders, only to be equally immobile when put back in its place. How absurd to cry for deliverance from distress to a god who "cannot answer" (v. 7).

Long before, Elijah, prophet of the Lord, in an all-day contest with 400 prophets of Baal, had proven beyond all doubt that the so-called gods cannot answer the cries of their worshippers. The terms of the contest had been agreed to: "the God who answers by fire, He is God." The prophets of Baal "called on the name of Baal . . . cried with a loud voice and cut themselves" all day long, "but there was no voice, no one answered, and no one paid attention." Then Elijah called, "Answer me, O Lord, answer me, that this people may know that You, O Lord, are God." "Then the fire of the Lord fell . . . and when the people saw it, they fell on their faces and said, 'The Lord, He is God'" (1 Kgs 24–39). David affirmed,

By awesome deeds You answer us in righteousness,
O God of our salvation (Ps 65:5).

On another occasion David reported,

I was crying to the Lord with my voice,
And He answered me from His holy mountain (Ps 3:4).

The Lord, Himself, said of the one who trusts in Him, "He will call upon Me, and I will answer him" (Ps 91:15).

46:8–13. Remember the Past; Look to the Future

Verses (46:) 8–10. In Isa 45:9–13 we found the exiled Jews "quarreling" with God concerning His plan to use Cyrus to free the exiles and re-inhabit Jerusalem. Again this "quarrel" is the focus of God's speech here. The people of God are called "transgressors" (v. 8). This accusation was brought against Israel repeatedly in the earlier chapters of Isaiah. But in spite of their earlier rebellions, God is still the one who "declares the end from the beginning . . . saying, 'My purpose will be established'" (v. 10).

"So you think My using Cyrus is highly unorthodox?" asks the Lord. Then "recall this to mind," "remember the former things," says the Lord. What "former things"? Remember, for example, that in former times I announced that I would "break Assyria in My land" (Isa 14:24–27). Remember that I predicted the subjugation of Egypt (Isa 19:11–16). These things I announced and they have come to pass. My record stands!

Verses (46:) 11–13. But exilic Israel is still "stubborn-minded" (v. 12). They want God to do things *their* way. They continue to be contemptuous of the Lord's plan to use Cyrus. But when Israel insists that the Lord shape the future to fit *her* understanding of the way things should be, she is behaving like an idolater. Idolaters can manipulate their idols to do or to appear to do *their* own will. But this attitude is unacceptable to God. God will not bend to Israel's stubborn beliefs. In any case, He has already called the "eagle from the east," Cyrus, "the man of My purpose" (v. 11).

And what of the future? Just as God announced and brought to pass historic events in the past, so He will do in the future. And He will do it *His* way—using Cyrus to "grant salvation in Zion, and My glory for Israel" (v. 13). Unorthodox? Perhaps. Unusual? No.

And this is a lesson not only for Israel of the past, but for us, God's people in the present. God does not always do things our way. In fact, He rarely does. Often, His invitation to us is, "Do you see what I am doing? Are you willing to let Me do this *My* way? If so, then come along and see the salvation of the Lord."

BABYLON, THE WIDOW (ISAIAH 47)

There are four units in Chapter 47:

☐ A taunt: From a Throne to the Dust (vv. 1–4).

☐ A taunt: From Glory to Darkness (vv. 5–7).

☐ A Bereaved Widow (vv. 8–11),

☐ No One to Save (vv. 12–15).

This chapter is a single poem containing four stanzas. The Lord speaks throughout, with perhaps a "choral response" in verses 4–5. Picking up scenes from Isaiah 46:1–2 and 45:20, the poem depicts Babylon claiming to be a god who will never fall—but Isaiah insists that it *will* fall, just like her idols. The poem vividly describes the extinction of the Babylonian empire, and gives the reason: *God's judgment.* This will happen in spite of all of Babylon's boasting of her wisdom, sorcery and astrological knowledge. The best of her human resources will fail, just as her gods will fail (chapter 46). *The biggest world empire known to that time will become only a historical memory!*

47:1–4. A Taunt—From a Throne to the Dust

Babylon is pictured as a delicate, refined princess, now reduced to the status of a slave girl, to "sit in the dust." The taunt promises that Babylon will never again enjoy the luxury of "a throne" (v. 1). The former princess must now earn her living as a servant, "grind[ing] meal" with "millstones." Servants cannot afford an expensive "veil" or "skirt." And, whereas as a princess, slaves carried her across streams in a carriage or chair, now she must cross on foot with uncovered legs (v. 2). At the level of slave, she is now subject to the indignity of "nakedness" (v. 3).

God's "vengeance" upon Babylon (v. 3) is seen as redemption for the Exiles—just as the plagues upon Egypt in the first Exodus were redemption for the enslaved Hebrews. Here, in the "choral response," rings out the characteristic name of the Lord: *Our Redeemer* (v. 4). Neither the idols of Babylon nor Persian Cyrus deserve this title. Only *the Lord* is the one who redeems!

47:5–7. A Taunt—From Glory to Darkness

Here is another sharp contrast. Babylon is depicted as the dethroned queen: she is no longer "Queen of Kingdoms" (v. 5). The structure of Babylon's empire was that of many small kingdoms, each swearing loyalty to the emperor. But now Babylon will descend from the glory of world domination into the "silence" and "darkness" of extinction (v. 5).

The Lord explains the reason why His people have been subject to Babylon for so long: He had been "angry with" them. So He "gave them" into Babylon's power. But the Lord also explains the reason why Babylon will now pass into historical memory. It was not just because Babylon had attacked and captured God's people, but because they showed excessive cruelty in doing so: they *showed no mercy on the aged!* (v. 6). Additionally is the charge of arrogance, believing herself to be divine: "I shall be Queen forever" (v. 7).

47:8–11. A Bereaved Widow

This taunting song describes a nation that views *itself* to be all that matters, rivaling God, even declaring, "I am, and there is no one besides me" (vv. 8, 10). Such arrogance cannot be tolerated, for it is only the Lord who may declare, "I am the Lord, and there is no other" (Isa 45:5, 6). Babylon's sense of false security (v. 8) was encouraged by her "sorceries" and "spells" (v. 9), and by her "wisdom" and "knowledge" (v. 10). So the great Queen would experience "loss of children and widowhood" at the same time (v. 9), two of the worst thing that could happen to a woman in the biblical world. Together they would mean loneliness and loss of protection. Babylon had lost all hope of support, and her demise would come "suddenly" (v. 9, 11).

47:12–15. No One to Save

The taunt continues. In your hour of crisis, O Babylon, you know only to continue doing what you have done "from your youth": "spells" and "sorceries" (v. 12). In your hour of crisis, is there anyone to save you? How about your "astrologers, those who prophesy by the stars, those who predict by the new moons"? Can they "save you from what will come upon you"? (v. 13). No? Then, how about those with whom you have traded and made alliances (v. 15)? Will they come to your aid? No. They will only be interested in saving themselves: "each has wandered in his own way."

No, when the judgment of "fire" (v. 14) comes upon you, there will be "none to save you" (v. 15).

Summary of Chapter 47

In this chapter, Babylon is depicted, first, *as the ultimate of national self-centeredness and self-deception, and of a nation that worships success and luxury.* Looking back, her pride and ambition are the ultimate symbol of human sin, portrayed by a people of a much earlier time, in the same location, who said, "Come, let us build for ourselves a city, and a tower whose top will reach into heaven, and let us make for ourselves a name, *lest we be scattered abroad over the face of the whole earth.*" Their great building enterprise did not succeed; their city became only a historical memory, for "the Lord scattered them abroad over the face of the whole earth" (Gen 11:1–9). Likewise, the Babylon of the sixth century B.C. determined to make a name for herself, but by *scattering herself abroad over the face of the whole earth.* In 6th century Babylon's case, the Lord reverses the pattern and removes her presence from the many kingdoms to which she has scattered herself, shrinking her to nothing but a conquered city, and that city then becoming nothing but a historical memory.

Second, Babylon is *the symbol of all humankind and its capacity for self-delusion, sinful pride and ambition,* as found in the later Romans and their city of Rome. John the Revelator symbolically calls their city "Babylon" and pronounces God's judgment against it: "And Babylon the great was remembered before God, to give her the cup of the wine of His fierce wrath" (Rev 16:19); again, "Woe, woe, the great city, Babylon, the strong city! For in one hour your judgment has come"; and again, "Thus will Babylon, the great city, be thrown down with violence, and will not be found any longer" (Rev 18:10, 21). As in the former Babylon of the sixth century B.C., whose trading and treaty partners deserted her in her time of crisis, Rome's trading partners, in

103

her hour of crisis, would "stand at a distance" and cry out, "Woe, woe, the great city . . . for in one hour she has been laid waste" (Rev 18:11–19).

Such is the suddenness of destruction that comes upon all men and women who live their lives in the context of sinful pride, self-delusion and ambition. In Psalm 73, the Psalmist speaks of the prosperous "wicked" (v. 3) who say, "How does God know?" (v. 11). Their end comes unexpectedly:

> Surely You set them in slippery places;
> You cast them down to destruction.
> How they are destroyed in a moment!
> They are utterly swept away by sudden terrors (Ps 73:18–19)

THE LORD'S GLORY (ISAIAH 48)

There are three major units in chapter 48:

- Prophecy, Past and Present (vv. 1–11).
- The Lord, First and Last (vv. 12–16).
- The Way of Peace and Prosperity (vv. 17–19).

This chapter opens with a court herald's call to a gathering of Exiles, "Hear this!" (v. 1). They are in court before the Lord. The chapter climaxes with the urgent command: "Go forth from Babylon! Flee from the Chaldeans!" (v. 20–21). In fact, all of chapters 40–47 have been leading up to this joyous announcement: *It is now time to go home!*

At the heart of this chapter are two major speeches by the Lord to the Exiles. In the first (vv. 3–11), the Lord summarizes the historical evidences that it is *He* who announces events before they take place, not any "idol" (v. 5). Yet Israel has been deliberately deaf, unreliable and rebellious (v. 8); she has refused to acknowledge these evidences. In the second, the Lord again defends His choice of Cyrus (vv. 12–15; see Isa 44:28; 45:13; 46:11), then concludes with an "if only" heart cry of what might have been if Israel's past response had been one of obedience (vv. 17–19).

48:1–11. Prophecy, Past and Present

The main argument of this section is that the Lord had long ago predicted the course of His people's history, so that, as events happened, His people would have no reason to attribute these events to any pagan idol or deity. Likewise, God is now about to do new things on the stage of world history, so He is predicting them, for the same reason.

Verses (48:) 1–6a look to *the past*. Two themes are interwoven: a reminder of Israel's stubborn past (vv. 1, 2, 4), and a reminder of how past prophecy has been fulfilled (vv. 3, 5, 6a).

In verses 1–2 the herald addresses the gathered Israelite exiles under five designations, first along *political and ethnic lines:* (1) "House of Jacob" is a general title for all those descended from the sons of Jacob. But it also refers more specifically to those of the ten tribes of the Northern Kingdom. (2) Those "who are named Israel" is broader; this would include historically those who, though not descendents of Jacob, as "a mixed multitude also went up with" Israel from Egyptian slavery (Exod 12:38). (3) Those "who came forth from the loins of Judah" addresses the main group of those who came from Judah to Babylon in the exile of 587 B.C. The herald then addresses them in terms of *religious affiliation:* (4) those "who swear by the name of the Lord" and (5) those "who invoke the God of Israel." The last designation could possibly include proselytes to the Jewish faith during the period of exile. Thus, these five designations make sure no one is overlooked.

Yet the charge in this courtroom scene is *insincerity*. Some of these gathered exiles, though they swear by the Lord's name (v. 1), and call themselves "From the Holy City" (v. 2), that is, true citizens of Jerusalem, and "lean upon the God of Israel" (v. 2) for whatever benefits may be gained, do so "neither in truth nor in righteousness" (v. 1). These are skeptics who find it convenient to be named among God's people, but neither truly believe in the Living God nor in His ability to deliver them from exile.

Following the naming of the defendants and the identifying of the charge against them, the Lord speaks. He speaks first of "the former things" (v. 3), which would include the great event of the first Exodus and all the subsequent events of Israel's history up to and including the Exile itself. Not only have "I proclaimed them," but also "I acted, and they came to pass" (v. 3). The Lord claims to be the (only) God who both speaks and acts. And if Israel would do so, she could testify to the truth of this: "You have heard . . . will you not declare it?" (v. 6).

Verses (48:) 6b–11 turn to *the present.* On the basis of the Lord's past record, the "new things" of this present prophecy—concerning Cyrus and the fall of Babylon—will be fulfilled. God will be faithful to His own character and will act to defend His own reputation (vv. 9, 11).

In contrast to God's faithfulness is Israel's past continual unfaithfulness: "your ear has not been open" (v. 8). This is a deliberate refusal to hear, defined so by the terms *treachery* and *rebellion,* signifying an attitude of the heart which Israel has had "since birth" (v. 8). Here is a link with the opening scene of Isaiah's prophecy, also a "trial" scene, where the Lord has called all the inhabitants of the heavens and earth to hear His charge against Israel:

> Sons I have reared and brought up,
> But they have *rebelled* against Me . . . .
> Sons who act corruptly!
> They have abandoned the Lord,
> They have despised the Holy One of Israel,
> They have turned away from Him (Isa 1:2–4).

In the face of such rebelliousness, we get an Old Testament glimpse of what the New Testament calls *grace*! The Lord could have brought instant judgment. Instead, He says, "I delay My wrath." Otherwise, I would have "cut you off" long before. But it was not any inherent righteousness in Israel that called forth God's grace, but rather, says God, it is "for the sake of My name . . . for My praise" (v. 9).[1]

God's alternative to instant judgment was a refining process, a testing "in the furnace of affliction" (v. 10). Such affliction began the moment God's people escaped from Egypt and continued right up to the final destruction of Jerusalem: hunger, thirst and wars in the wilderness; oppressions by enemies in the times of the Judges; famines, earthquakes, invasions by enemy nations in the days of the kingdom. The final "furnace of affliction" was the Exile to Babylon, a return to slave status, just as they had been long ago in Egypt. What had this long history of refining produced? Silver? No, "not as silver" (v. 10). Earlier in Isaiah's prophecy, the Lord has said, "Your silver has become dross"—the dross of murder, thievery and bribery, resulting in injustice to orphans and widows (Isa 1:21–23). But, says God, "I . . . will smelt away your dross . . . and you will be called the 'City of Righteousness,' a faithful city" (Isa 1:25–26).

---

[1] In the closing days of Judah's existence as a sovereign nation, the prophet Ezekiel likewise reviewed God's longstanding grace, going way back to the days of Egyptian bondage: (1) even in Egypt "they rebelled . . . they did not forsake the idols of Egypt . . . . I resolved to pour out my wrath on them . . . but I acted for the sake of My name . . . by bringing them out of the land of Egypt" (Ezek 20:8–9); (2) then they "rebelled against me in the wilderness . . . then I resolved to pour out My wrath on them in the wilderness to annihilate them. But I acted for the sake of My name . . . [and] My eye spared them rather than destroying them" (Ezek 20:13–17).

Such smelting away of Israel's dross will be a pure act of grace! She does not deserve it. She cannot remove it herself. But her final "furnace of affliction" has ended. The judgment of exile is complete. Therefore, says God, "For My own sake, for My own sake, I will act" (v. 11).

But the Lord has one final statement to make in this courtroom speech of historical evidences: "My glory I will not give to another" (v. 11). Here is a warning to the exiles that they dare not say, "My idol has done them"(v. 5), as their forefathers had done at the foot of Mt. Sinai long ago (Exod 32:4). God refuses to let idols take credit for His past judgments upon His people or for the act of redemption He is about to do.

48:12–16. The Lord, First and Last

Again the Lord speaks. In verses 12–13 the Lord exalts and asserts Himself through a repetition of three earlier themes: (1) God's uniqueness, "I am the first, I am also the last" (v. 12; see Isa 41:4; 43:10, 13; 46:4), (2) God as Creator, "My hand founded the earth . . . spread out the heavens" (v. 13; see Isa 42:5; 45:12, 18), and (3) God's astonishing call of Cyrus, " I have called him" (v. 15; compare Isa 41:2; 45:1–3).

Verse 14 appears to be an interruption by the prophet who gives a remarkable addition to what has already been said about Cyrus as God's shepherd (Isa 44:28) and anointed one (Isa 45:1): "The Lord loves him" (v. 14). Cyrus is the one whom God has chosen and who will do His will.

The Lord emphasizes His personal involvement in calling Cyrus and "mak[ing] his ways successful" (v. 15), just as He was personally involved in the creation of earth and heaven. The God who is Israel's Redeemer (v. 17) is not some aloof, uninvolved deity who set the universe in place and then retired to some far off place, unconcerned about the course and outcome of history. Rather, He is a living personal God, hearing, speaking, calling—unlike the idols who neither hear nor speak—creating and sustaining the universe, raising up and bringing down kings, directing history, even the history of a small and insignificant people called Israel!

48:17–19. The Way of Peace and Prosperity

If God is truly as He is described in verses 12–16 (and He is!) then His way is the only dependable and profitable way to follow. If His people will allow Him, God promises that He is the one "who leads you in the way you should go," and along that way "teaches you to profit" (v. 17).

"Profit" as used here is in direct contrast to Isaiah's use of . the term in three contexts that negate the profit that idols and magic promise (Isa 44:9–10; 47:12; 57:12), and in one context that negates the profit that an alliance with a foreign nation promises (Isa 30:1–5).[2] No idol, no trick of magic, and certainly not Pharaoh, could make good on a promise to benefit the people of God. But the Living God not only promises, he delivers great benefits to those who walk in His way.

And lest God's people, in their ignorance, are unable to recognize either the true way of the Lord or the benefits of walking in His way, the Lord is ready to "teach" them. Here is a link with an earlier reference of Isaiah to the Lord as "Teacher"

---

[2] In this instance, an earlier intention of Judah to make an alliance with Egypt and its king Pharaoh, who was considered by the Egyptians to be a god; thus an alliance with Pharaoh was tantamount to making a covenant with another god!

of His way: "He, your Teacher will no longer hide Himself, but your eyes will behold your Teacher. And your ears will hear a word behind you, 'This is the way, walk in it,' whenever you turn to the right or to the left." And if God's people throw away their "graven images" as an "impure thing," the profit of walking in God's way is real and knowable: "rain" to make their seed grow, "bread" from the abundant "yield of the ground," "roomy pasture" for their livestock, "salted fodder" for their oxen and donkeys (Isa 30:19–24).

But alas! Israel had not "paid attention" to the commandments of the Lord (v. 18). She had *not* walked in God's way. Oh, if only she had, then her "peace" (well-being) would have been ongoing "like a river" and her "righteousness" (right-being) would have continued like the never ceasing "waves of the sea" (v. 18). And instead of her "offspring" being cut off (in exile), they would have multiplied like the grains of sand (v. 19). Here is clear reference to the promise made to Abraham (Gen 13:16; 15:5; 22:17), and to the linking of the fulfillment of promise to obedience.

"If only" God's people could see the direct line from *promise* to *obedience* to *fulfillment*. But human sin, weakness of faith, and personal ambition lead down so many side paths, that fulfillment is delayed, and delayed, and sometimes not realized at all. So it was in the case of exiled Israel.

In the first century A.D., the Galatian church likewise seemed in danger of missing the fulfillment of the divine promise. Thus Paul wrote to them, "You were running well; who hindered you from obeying the truth?" (Gal 5:7). You are "Abraham's offspring, heirs according to promise" (Gal 3:29). You have been sidetracked by "some who are disturbing you" by preaching "a different gospel" (Gal 1:6–7). This diversion from the "Gospel of Christ" had led to backbiting (Gal 5:15), boastfulness and envy (Gal 5:26), and other "deeds of the flesh" (Gal 5:19–21) among the Galatian Christians, thus delaying the Spirit's fulfillment in them that should result from obedience to the truth: "love, joy, peace, patience, kindness, goodness, faithfulness, gentleness, self-control" (Gal 5:22–23). And, just as Isaiah characterized the Old Testament Israelite's obedience as walking in God's way, so Paul characterizes the New Testament Christian's obedience as "walking by the Spirit," "being led by the Spirit," "living by the Spirit," and "following the Spirit" (Gal 5:16, 18, 25).

"If only" we Christians in the twenty-first century A.D. Church could fully learn to walk the path of obedience to God's Spirit and Word, God would fulfill in us a spiritual well-being and right-being that would produce spiritual offspring beyond measure.

48:20–22. Go Home!

But we must return to the exiles gathered in Babylon. They have heard the court herald twice call out, "Now hear this!" (vv. 1, 12). They have heard the Lord speak, re-confirming Himself and His call of Cyrus. Now they hear what many have long been waiting for: "Go forth from Babylon!" It's now time to go home![3]

---

[3] Ezra-Nehemiah tell of four expeditions of returnees in three periods led by Sheshbazzar (Ezra 1:5–11), Zerubabbel (Ezra 2:2–69), Ezra (Ezra 7:1–8; 8:1–32)) and Nehemiah (Neh 2:1–11). Each group of returnees went with the authority of a royal Persian edict to rebuild the Temple, and finally the walls

The year is probably 538 B.C., the year of Emperor Cyrus's decree concerning "everyone whose spirit God had stirred to go up and rebuild the house of the Lord, which is in Jerusalem." This was a *spiritual* venture in the flesh. That is, only those into whose hearts *God* had put the desire to go were to join this initial expedition, under the leadership of Sheshbazzar, "the prince of Judah" (see Ezra 1:5–11). This first group of returnees was no doubt rather few in number, but they had been entrusted with the 5,400 precious utensils that had been robbed from Solomon's Temple by Babylonian Nebuchadnezzar's armies.

The journey would not be easy. They would be traveling through unknown territory, food and water might be hard to obtain. Drawing upon terms of the first Exodus, Isaiah reports that God will be marching right along with His people. They need not fear!

> And they did not thirst when He led them through the deserts.
> He made the water flow out of the rock for them;
> He split the rock, and the water gushed forth (v. 21).

Would these returnees be opposed by those already living in Judea, as the Israelites had been in the first Exodus? Joyous word is sent ahead to the first checkpoints to be approached in Palestine: "The Lord has redeemed His servant Jacob!" (v. 20).

---

of Jerusalem. The task would not be completed for nearly 100 years, but God had planned it, declared it, and now He acts to set the plan in motion.

SING, O HEAVENS! BE JOYFUL, O EARTH! (ISAIAH 49)

This chapter will be discussed in three major units:

- ❑ The Servant: Called to Redeem His People (vv. 1–6).
- ❑ Israel's Restoration (vv. 7–13).
- ❑ Zion Is Reassured (vv. 14–26).

Chapters 49—55 comprise the second half of Isaiah's prophecy to the Exiles in Babylon. Several themes that appeared throughout the first half, chapters 40–48, are absent in this second half: (1) there is no further reference to Babylon or Cyrus; (2) there are no more attacks on worship of idols; (3) there are no more court cases; (4) there are no more appeals to earlier prophecies and their fulfillment. Instead, Isaiah's address is now mainly directed to Zion/Jerusalem, rather than to Jacob/Israel. It is as though God's act of redemption from Babylonian captivity is viewed as "accomplished." Thus, Isaiah's main concern now is with the rebuilding and re-inhabiting of Jerusalem. But Isaiah also now looks further down the road of human history—The Lord will bring about an even greater deliverance than that from Babylon. He will deliver His people from the sin that caused their bondage. He will accomplish this through the Messiah, the ideal Servant. Thus, Isaiah's depictions of the "Servant" will find their ultimate fulfillment in Jesus Christ.

49:1–6. The Second "Servant Song". The Servant: Called to Redeem His People

The Servant speaks here in the first person about Himself, His mission and His experience. He addresses, not Israel, but the "coastlands/peoples from afar" (v. 1), showing the universal scope of God's intended salvation. God's salvation is for "the nations" (v. 6).

The Servant emphasizes His divine election and appointment, even before His birth: "The Lord called me from the womb" (v. 1). This, in itself, is not unique to the biblical record; both Jeremiah (Jer 1:5) and John the Baptist (Luke 1:15) were called while yet in their mother's womb. But in light of the mission to which the Servant is appointed, this is perhaps a prophetic reference to the Virgin Birth of Jesus.

God's servant is fully equipped for His mission (v. 2). The emphasis here is on the *verbal* nature of His ministry: "My mouth." His teaching will be effective since it is described as a weapon, "a sword" or "a sharpened arrow." The focus is on the effective power of the Word of God. Earlier, Isaiah, in speaking of the "Shoot . . . from the stem of Jesse," a reference to the future Messiah, says,

> He will strike the earth with the rod of His mouth,
> And with the breath of His lips He will slay the wicked
> (Isa 11:4).

Jeremiah says, "Is not My Word like fire? declares the Lord, and like a hammer which shatters a rock?" (Jer 23:29).

The author of Hebrews declares, "The word of God is living and active and sharper than any two-edged sword" (Heb 4:12).

Yet, there is a "hidden" aspect to the Servant's ministry (v. 2). This suggests that the effectiveness of His ministry will be indirect, rather than a direct or violent attack. There is a parallel here with the parabolic method of Jesus, and His teaching on the "hiddenness" of the Kingdom of God.

The Servant claims that His identity and status are from God Himself:

> He said to me, "You are my Servant, Israel,
> In whom I will show My glory" (v. 3).

This proclamation has the same royal overtones as in Ps 2:7:

> He said to Me, "You are My Son,
> Today I have begotten You,"

or earlier in Isaiah 42:1:

> Behold, My Servant, whom I uphold;
> My chosen one in whom My soul delight.

The Servant claims that God has designated Him as one "in whom I will show My glory" (v. 3). This is a unique privilege. Such a thing has never been said of any previous individual prophet or servant of God.

Since this song seems clearly individual from the beginning, the sudden identification of the Servant as corporate "Israel" (v. 3) at first seems problematic. How can the individual servant actually be called "Israel"? Does "Israel" have a mission to Israel? The problem disappears, however, when we see that the attitudes expressed in verse 4 are not those of the nation of Israel. Rather, this Person is the ideal Israel, One who embodies within Himself what Israel might have been. The future Messiah has a mission *to* Israel, then *beyond* Israel to the other "nations" (v. 6).

In contrast to what God has said to the Servant, the Servant said, "I have toiled in vain" (v. 4). The Servant considers that His mission to Israel has been a failure. It involved great struggle and effort, but seemed to have achieved no results—"I have spent my strength for nothing" (v. 4). Yet he leaves the matter "with the Lord," in whose hands He believes is "justice" and "reward" (v. 4). A characteristic of this Servant, seen more clearly in Isaiah 53, is His refusal to defend Himself, even in the face of injustice and opposition. From a human point of view Jesus' ministry ended in failure, but he never resorted to human efforts to gain worldly success. Peter, in holding up Jesus' attitude for Christians to follow who are under persecution, comments: *while being reviled, He did not revile in return; while suffering, He uttered no threats, but kept entrusting Himself to Him who judges righteously (1 Pet 2:23).* This is also a good habit for Christians to cultivate in ordinary, everyday life!

The Lord's response to the Servant's despair and sense of failure is "But now . . . " (v. 5). The Lord now gives Him an even wider and greater mission, beyond the mission "to bring Jacob back" (v. 5); He is to be "a light to the nations" (v. 6). The Servant *is* given the mission to bring Israel back to God, but like the prophets of Israel for whom this was their constant mission, He too will experience rejection in His mission. Thus He will be entrusted with the larger mission of bringing "salvation to the ends of the earth" (v. 6). Jesus spoke rather pointedly of this rejection of the "son" by Israel in the parable of the wicked tenant farmers. The kingdom of God, that is, the offer of salvation, would be taken from Israel and "given to a nation producing the fruit of it" (Matt 21:32–46).

A Brief History of "Servant" Theology

Before continuing our study of Isaiah 49, a brief discussion of the history of the interpretation of Isaiah's "Servant" theology is needed. Following our study of chapter 42, I gave a brief summary of the "Servant" theology up to that point in our study. The main points were: (1) the first picture of the servant is

117

collective Israel whom God intended, through obedient servanthood, to show the rest of the world God's true pattern for humanity; (2) collective Israel, however, was a failed servant—spiritually blind and deaf; (3) God, therefore, could not fulfill His purpose through Israel; (4) the second picture of the Servant is of the individual figure, distinct from Israel, with ultimate fulfillment in Jesus Christ.

I discussed above the opening verses of chapter 49 in which the Servant is called to redeem God's people, and indicated that the servant terminology in these verses points to the Messiah, Jesus Christ.

Before the era of modern biblical criticism (which began in the late eighteenth century among European biblical scholars), Christian writers, with few exceptions, interpreted Isaiah's Servant Songs as messianic prophecies, pointing to an individual royal, but suffering, Messiah, fulfilled in Jesus. In the pre-Christian era (the time between the Old and New Testaments), Jewish rabbinic scholars also identified the servant with an individual Messiah, but they removed all references to his suffering; he was to be some political figure, who would "restore the kingdom to Israel" (see Acts 1:6). In the early Christian era, controversy with the Christians caused the rabbis to set aside this identification; the servant then became identified with the (messianic) nation Israel.

Among modern liberal Christian scholars, and even among many who would call themselves "evangelical," the identification of the servant with the individual Jesus Christ has also been virtually abandoned. Some, still favoring an individualistic interpretation, identify the servant with some historical Old Testament figure, such as Moses, Zerubbabel, Jeremiah, Hezekiah or Cyrus. Some propose even the author of the Servant Songs himself, a supposed unknown prophet to whom they refer as "Second Isaiah." The favorite theory, however, is that the servant is to be identified with Israel as a collective entity, or at least a faithful remnant within Israel, or perhaps the Israelite prophets as a group.

Objections to the collective theory are many. Two are: (1) the description of the servant in the songs is given in very individualistic terms: he is anointed with the Spirit of God (Isa 42:1); he is called while still in his mother's womb (Isa 49:1); he gives his back to those who strike him and his cheeks to those who pluck out the beard [50:6]; his grave is with the wicked (Isa 53:9); (2) Isaiah does not credit the sufferings of Israel in exile to the sins of others (and thus vicariously suffering on behalf of others), but as God's judgment upon her for her own rebellion against Him and continual violation of the covenant. Therefore, the one(s) suffering in Isaiah 42:24–25 cannot be the same as the One suffering in Isaiah 53:6–9.

> Who gave Jacob up for spoil, and Israel to plunderers?
> Was it not the Lord, against whom we [=Israel] have sinned,
> And in whose ways they [=Israel] were not willing to walk,
> And whose law they did not obey?
> So He [=the Lord] poured out on him [=Israel] the heat of His anger
> And the fierceness of battle;
> And it set him aflame all around,
> Yet he did not recognize it;
> And it burned him, but he paid no attention (Isa 42:24–25)
> All of us [=Israel] like sheep have gone astray,
> Each of us has turned to his own way;
> But the Lord has caused the iniquity of us all
> To fall upon Him [=the Servant].
> He [=the Servant] was oppressed and afflicted. . .
> He was cut off out of the land of the living,

119

> For the transgression of My [i.e., God's] people [=Israel] He
> was stricken . . . (Isa 53:6–9).

The Servant must be identified as one unlike any other figure pictured elsewhere in the Old Testament. The portrayal of the Servant was suited well to the life and ministry of Jesus. He refused to be the type of political revolutionary leader that the Jews wanted Him to be. Rather, the servant became the model through which He carried out his mission—salvation for the whole world. In Him two Old Testament streams of thought flowed together to become one. If only Israel had eyes opened to see, she would surely have seen the One who brought together in Himself both Messiah and Suffering Servant It was not by human design that Jesus was proclaimed king while "He Himself bore our sins in His body on the cross, that we might die to sin and live to righteousness" (1 Pet 2:24).

The various aspects of Isaiah's prophecy of the Messiah, and their fulfillment in the New Testament is shown in **Table 1: Isaiah's Prophecy and Its Fulfillment in NT** on page 167.

49:7–13. Israel's Restoration

God now speaks, identifying Himself as both "Redeemer of Israel" and "Holy One"(v. 7) The title "Redeemer" emphasizes God's work of salvation (see also my comments on Isa 41:14), while the title "Holy One" emphasizes God's work of judgment. That is, Israel will be set free, but Israel's oppressors will be punished.

To whom does God speak here? Is it to the Servant-Messiah of verses 1–6 whose assignment extends to the whole world, or to (failed) servant Israel still in exile in Babylon? Some see verse 7 as part of the previous Servant Song of verses 1–6; thus the one addressed is the Servant-Messiah. Others see it as part of the succeeding word to Israel in verses 8–13; thus the one addressed is Israel in exile. I follow the second view. Thus, after his interlude of giving us a glimpse of the future worldwide work of the Servant-Messiah, Isaiah brings us back to where he left Israel at the end of chapter 48, still in exile in Babylon.

Yet the future work of the anticipated Servant-Messiah is not unrelated to the present exile and soon-to-come deliverance and restoration of Israel, for the redemptive work of Jesus Christ is effective not only from the Cross onward, but also from the Cross backward to the very beginning of history. Jesus is "the Lamb slain from the foundation of the world" (Rev 13:8, NKJV). Thus, in a mystery too hidden for us to fully grasp, the work of the restoration of Israel from Babylon to Zion is a work of the Servant-Messiah. His blessings extend backward from the Cross, even to exiled and suffering Israel.

O Israel, says the Lord, you are indeed "the despised one," "the one abhorred by the nations," nothing but a "servant of rulers" (v. 7); your land lies "desolate" (v. 8), you are the "afflicted" (v. 13). But your suffering and humiliation will soon come to an end. "Kings" and "princes," (v. 7) when they see that you have been restored, will "bow down" (v. 7). Before Israel? Yes (see Isa 49:23), but in truth before the incomparable God, the "Holy One of Israel," who has brought about her return to Zion. For Israel's humiliation has not been simply because she had gone into exile, but because of the seemingly *ineffectiveness of her God* to keep her in the land of Israel when faced with powerful foreign nations. This humiliation is reflected in Psalm 137:

> By the rivers of Babylon,
> There we sat down and wept,
> When we remembered Zion.

121

Upon the willows in the midst of it
We hung our harps.
For there our captors demanded of us songs,
And our tormentors mirth, saying,
"Sing us one of the songs of Zion" (Ps 137: 1–3).

Emphasizing the security of Jerusalem, now in the exiles' present captivity, the songs of Zion seem empty. Their captors' demand that they sing these songs is no source of comfort; it is a taunt that cuts to the soul. Also, Psalm 80, though possibly associated with the exile of the northern Israelite tribes following the fall of Samaria in 721 B.C., likewise reflects this feeling of humiliation:

O Lord God of hosts,
How long will You be angry with the prayers of Your people?
You have fed them with the bread of tears,
And You make us an object of contention to our neighbors;
And our enemies laugh among themselves.
O God of hosts, restore us,
And cause Your face to shine upon us,
And we will be saved (Ps 80:4–7).

Yes, exiled Israel's humiliation will soon end. Why? Because of Israel's goodness? No. Because of the Lord's faithfulness! The Lord "has chosen" Israel, long before, while still in her previous humiliation in Egyptian bondage, and He has not negated that choice (v. 7).

Israel in exile has heard the command: "Go forth from Babylon!" (Isa 48:20). The journey will not be easy. They will be traveling through unknown territory, food and water might be hard to obtain. The command is now repeated:

To those who are bound, "Go forth,"
To those who are in darkness, "Show yourselves" (v. 9).

122

Our Incomparable God

The journey back to Zion is pictured in some detail in verses 8–12, using language that echoes the first Exodus. Israel had cried out in despair (implied) and God has "answered" (v. 8; see Exod 2:23–25). God leads them like a shepherd, providing pasture for feeding along the way (v. 9; see Deut 1:31; 2:7); He "guides them to springs of water" (v. 10; see Exod 17:6). In a metaphor familiar from Isaiah 40:3–4, God prepares a highway for easier traveling (v. 11). Note that God says, "*My* mountains." Because He made them, he can also transform them into mere "roads." Who will be traveling on these God-prepared roads? Not only those Israelites from Babylon (the east), but exiled Israelites from the far corners of the earth—from "the north and the west" and from the south—Sinim, perhaps a name for Syene to the south of Egypt (v. 12).

Isaiah cannot help but respond to such gracious deeds of the Lord. He bursts forth into a hymn of praise, calling the heavens, earth and mountains also to "break forth into joyful shouting" in view of the Lord's comfort and compassion upon "His afflicted" (v. 13). Even this hymn of praise is a reminder of the hymn of praise that Moses and the Israelites sang after God's great deliverance from the Egyptians at the Red Sea:

> I will sing to the Lord, for He is highly exalted . . . .
> The Lord is my strength and song,
> And He has become my salvation . . .
> Your right hand, O Lord, shatters the enemy . . .
> Who is like You among the gods, O Lord?
> Who is like You, majestic in holiness,
> Awesome in praises, working wonders? . . .
> In Your lovingkindness You have led the people whom You
>   have redeemed;
> In Your strength You have guided them to Your holy
>   habitation.
> The peoples have heard, they tremble . . . .

123

The Lord shall reign forever and ever (Exod 15:1–18).

49:14–26. Zion is Reassured

This lengthy passage contains three sections, each built around a complaint of "Zion," to which God responds. Here Zion is used figuratively for the exiles themselves who will soon be going back to re-inhabit Jerusalem.

Verses (49:) 14–18: First Complaint. In words of an abandoned wife, the people accuse God of being an unfaithful husband: "The Lord has forsaken me" (v. 14). This is indeed ironical in that other prophets accuse Israel of being the unfaithful wife! See, for example, Ezek 16:32: *"You adulteress wife, who takes strangers instead of her husband,"*

or,

> How lonely sits the city
> That was full of people!
> She has become like a widow . . .
> She has none to comfort her
> Among all her lovers . . . (Lam 1:1–2).

God replies with a different metaphor—that of a mother's love. A mother's love for the child that came from her own "womb," that "nurses" at her own breast (v. 15), is stronger than even that between a husband and wife, yes, stronger than any other form of human love. And though there are mothers who prove to be the exception and abandon their children (see Lam 2:20; 4:10), "I will never forget you," says God. Indeed, how can God forget Israel when He has her "engraved on [His] palms" (v. 16)? The metaphor here is not that of a pen and ink drawing upon paper or parchment, which could easily be erased or blotted over, but of incising or scratching with an engraving tool into the surface of a brick (see Ezek 4:1), a broken piece of

124

pottery or a stone. "Such a thing I have done on my own hands—an incised sketch of the 'walls' of Jerusalem. The scars are permanent. How can I forget you, when you are 'continually before me' (v. 16)? As often as I look at my own hands, I think of you!"

Here is one of the most beautiful "love" passages in the Old Testament. Some modern-day interpreters insist on depicting God in the Old Testament as an unloving God, in opposition to a loving God in the New Testament. But this is a defective view. God's unfailing love, that drives Him again and again to woo His people back to Himself (see Hos 2:14–15), is that which binds both Testaments together.

Verses 17–18 describes the rebuilding and repopulation of Jerusalem as God sees it from the divine perspective. The rebuilding is being done in haste (v. 17) for those returnees already on the move from the four corners of the earth (v. 12). In an interesting play on a word, in Hebrew "your builders" (v. 17) may also be read "your sons." Thus, while most of those who went into exile will not have lived to see the miraculous rebuilding of Zion, their *sons* will return to be Zion's *builders*.

There is yet one more beautiful metaphor in this section—that of a bride adorning herself with "jewels" to enhance her beauty on her wedding day (v. 18). Zion is to "lift up [her] eyes" and see her children streaming to her from all directions along those roadways that God has prepared through the mountains (v. 11). Her *children* will be her bridal ornaments, enhancing the nation's beauty. The metaphor here is that of *re*-adornment. Only a wife (or wife-to-be) may wear the ornaments of marriage. And God, Israel's husband, has never died, He has never truly forsaken her. Just as God did for a time after Israel's sin with the golden calf in the days of Moses He has said to

Israel in exile, "Put off your ornaments from you, that I may know what I will do with you" (Exod 33:5). And now God has determined what He will do: He will again take Israel as His wife. It is time for *re*-adornment!

Verses (49:) 19–23: Second Complaint (implied): The "land" of Judah/Jerusalem is nothing but "waste and desolate places" (v. 19). Isaiah gives a graphic picture of just such an earlier desolation, following the invasion of Judah by Assyria's army in 701 B.C.

> Your land is desolate,
> Your cities burned with fire,
> Your fields—strangers are devouring them in your presence,
> It is desolation, as overthrown by strangers (Isa 1:7).

Perhaps the exiles are now asking, "How can we live in such a place? How can we ever again fill it? How will we ever again build up its towns, fields and vineyards?"

God's answer is that the land will be much too small to contain the many returning "children," so much so that *they* will complain, "This place is too cramped for me" (v 20). Zion, so long without children will be amazed and wonder, "Who has fathered these for me? . . . From where did these come?" (v. 20).

To this question of wonderment, the Lord answers, "I will lift up My hand to the nations" (v. 22) an expression for giving a command. The nations who have held captives from Israel will, themselves, bring them home to Zion. Metaphorically, the captives are pictured as young children that must be carried "in the bosom" or "on the shoulders" (v. 22). The "kings" and "princesses" whom they once served will now serve Israel, accompanying them on the long and dangerous journey as "guardians" and "nurses." In fact, they will even "bow down . . . with their faces [lit. noses!] to the ground" and kiss the feet

126

of their former slaves—all this depicting a great divine reversal. Notice yet again the motive behind this great reversal: *You [=Israel] will know* that I am the Lord (v. 23).

Verses (49:) 24–26: Third Complaint. "Can the prey [=Exiles] be taken from the mighty man [=Babylon]?" (v. 24). The question is: *Is God able?* The exiles must have felt themselves to be like a mouse caught in the claws of a lion. How could they ever dream of being freed from the world empire of Babylon? The answer is that the impossible will become the possible, based on a promissory word of God. In the Hebrew of verse 25, the pronoun "I" stands at the beginning of the last two lines, a position of emphasis:

> *I* will contend with the one who contends with you,
> And *I* will save your children.

Therefore, Israel will be rescued just as surely as God is God. Here is another of God's great reversals. And, again, what is its purpose? It now becomes universal:

> *All humanity will know* that I, the Lord, am your Savior
> And your Redeemer, the Mighty One of Jacob (v. 26).

TRUST IN THE NAME OF THE LORD!
(ISAIAH 50)

This chapter has three major units:

- ❏ Israel Separated, but not Divorced (vv. 1–3).
- ❏ The Third Servant Song: The Servant as Learner and Teacher (vv. 4–9).
- ❏ Encouragement and Judgment (vv. 10–11).

50:1–3. Israel Separated, but Not Divorced

Again, a court hearing conducted by the Lord is the context here. The Lord uses two metaphors drawn from Israel's social life (v. 1). The first is that of *divorce*. This present generation of exiles has apparently complained that the Lord (Israel's Husband) had, without just reason, divorced their "mother"—the previous generation—and sent her away into exile. Thus, they, her children, are in exile because of God's unjust act. The legal context for divorce is written in Deuteronomy 24:1–4, where God instructs Israel that if a man divorced his wife he must "write her a certificate of divorce and put it in her hand" before sending her "out from his house." On the basis of this law, the Lord challenges the exiles' complaint, demanding, "Where is the certificate of divorce, / By which I have sent your mother away?" (v. 1). The question is rhetorical, of course, for Israel in exile can produce no such document, in which case there has never been any divorce—only an estrangement, a break in the relationship, a separation.

The second metaphor is that of *debt-slavery*, whereby if a father fell into non-repayable debt, it was legally permissible for him to sell his children to the creditor to work off the debt (see Exod 21:7–11; Deut 15:12–14; Neh 5:1–12). Could it be possible that the Lord was in debt to someone and unable to repay, thus having to resort to selling His very own family members? How preposterous! "To whom of my creditors did I sell you?" (v. 1). How could God be a debtor to anybody? Who could possibly be the creditor of the Lord?

No, Israel had not been divorced arbitrarily. She had not been sold into debt-slavery. She had been "sold," however, but for her own "iniquities" and "transgressions" (v. 1). There had been no other reason.

Israel's sin is further clarified by the Lord's question in verse 2:

> Why was there no man when I came?
> When I called, why was there none to answer?

When I came to you in the past, speaking through My prophets, no one responded. My gracious overtures were ignored. "Return to me," I called, but among you there was dead silence. Even now you do not respond to the prophets' call, "Go forth" (Isa 49:9). Is there no one getting up to move out? Do you still disbelieve?

A second implied complaint of exiled Israel is that the Lord had run out of strength, had become old and weak, no longer capable of redeeming His people as He had in the past. This implied accusation is quickly denied:

> Is My hand so short that it cannot ransom?
> Or have I no power to deliver? (v. 2).

129

The implication is that any delay in Israel's redemption from slavery has been caused by her own disobedience. This is clearly stated later in Isaiah 59:1–2.

> Behold, the Lord's hand is not short that it cannot save;
> Neither is His ear so dull that it cannot hear.
> But your iniquities have made a separation between you and your God,
> And your sins have hid His face from you, so that He does not hear.

To prove His ability to do the seemingly impossible on behalf of His people, God cites a few instances of works of power that He can perform (v. 2). A sharp word of rebuke, and He can "dry up the sea," as He did through Moses at the Red Sea in the days of the first Exodus from Egypt (see Isa 17:13; Job 38:11; Ps 104:7; 106:9 for other instances of similar rebukes). With equal ease He can "make the rivers a wilderness." And to add a bit of color, in the beds of the dried up rivers we see the mass of fish, squirming and dying and stinking. Furthermore, God can "clothe the heavens with blackness," just as He brought the plague of darkness upon Egypt, also in the days of the first Exodus. This last example may also be pointing to the future, when the great judgment of God will fall upon the earth (see Joel 2:30–31; Acts 2:19–20), for "sackcloth," mentioned as the "covering" that God drapes over the heavens to shut out the light of the heavenly bodies, is a sign of sorrow and suffering. Thus, even the heavens must suffer when the Lord shows the grandeur of His power as the final Judge of all things.

Now, what is the point of all this? *That it will be no more difficult for God to redeem Israel from Babylonian slavery than it is to control all of nature or to deliver Israel from Egypt!*

50:4–9. The Third Servant Song

Once again the Servant himself speaks in the first person. We see further development of His character as a *perfect learner* and a *perfect teacher.*

The Servant has received from God the double gift of "the tongue of learners" and the "ear of learners" (v. 4). All his hearing and speaking are focused on God. His ears are opened (v. 5), a symbol of obedient submission. He does not speak to others without first hearing from God. This willingness to be taught has not come to the Servant automatically, however, for it has been necessary for the Lord to waken his ear "morning by morning" that he might learn (v. 4).

This gift enables the Servant "to sustain the weary one with a word" (v. 4). Who are these weary ones? According to Isaiah 49:5–6, the Servant's mission is to both Israel and the Gentiles. Thus the "weary" are to be found in both groups: Israelites laboring under the burden of the law and finding no peace, and Gentiles laboring under the burden of idol worship and likewise finding no peace. The "word" given by the Servant "to sustain the weary" finds its ultimate fulfillment in the gracious gospel of Jesus Christ, "Come unto Me, all who are weary and heavy laden, and I will give you rest" (Matt 11:28).

But in fulfilling his ministry to the weary, the Servant suffers ill-treatment, contempt and suffering.

> I gave My back to those who strike Me,
> And My cheeks to those who pluck out the beard;
> I did not cover My face from humili tion and spitting (v.6).

Here is a remarkably accurate description of the experience of Jesus at His trial.

Yet, out of his suffering the Servant finds confident expectation of vindication from God Himself (vv. 7–9). The

Servant invites his attackers into court to contend against him. Though they will be sure that they are on God's side, in fact God will declare the verdict against them and in favor of the Servant (vv. 8–9).

50:10–11. Encouragement and Judgment

These final two verses reinforce the words of the Servant. There is encouragement to those who decide to trust God and follow his Servant, even in the darkness of suffering (v. 10). But there is a warning of judgment to those who decide to follow their own way and walk in their own light (v. 11). The Servant confronts his listeners with two alternatives: either walk in the light of faith, or perish in the fires of destruction. These two alternatives still confront us today. Which do you choose?

THE RANSOMED OF THE LORD WILL
RETURN (ISAIAH 51)

This chapter has four major units:

- ☐ Victory, Deliverance and Righteousness (vv. 1–8).
- ☐ History and Eschatology (vv. 9–11).
- ☐ The Lord's Reassuring Answer (vv. 12–16).
- ☐ The Cup of God's Anger (vv. 17–23).

51:1–8. Victory, Deliverance and Righteousness

Isaiah now turns to a meditation on different aspects of God's righteousness, a meditation presented in a song with three distinct stanzas. Each stanza begins with "Listen to me!" (vv. 1, 4, 7), and each ends on a note of praise (vv. 3, 6, 8). The song gives a message of comfort (v. 3), a message first introduced in Isaiah 40:1 and repeated in Isaiah 49:13, and assurance concerning the certainty of the coming deliverance, addressed to the faithful among the Israelite exiles. We know they are the faithful because it is said that they are those "who pursue righteousness, who seek the Lord" (v. 1), that they are the offspring of Abraham and Sarah (v. 2), that they are the Lord's people (v. 4), and that they are those "who know righteousness" and in whose heart resides the law of God (v. 7).

Isaiah addresses this whole song, then, to those who pursue "righteousness" (v. 1). The Hebrew word (*tsedaqah*) can equally mean "deliverance." Perhaps Isaiah is being purposely ambiguous, allowing for two shades of meaning: "You who pursue after what is right," that is, who do justice (even in exile), and "You who are longing for deliverance" (from exile). Ultimately both are true, for God's deliverance inspires and requires right behavior. And both are summed up in the parallel line, "Who seek the Lord" (v. 1).

In the first stanza (vv. 1–3) Isaiah urges the exiles to "look to the rock . . . and to the quarry" from which they originally came (v. 1). Abraham and Sarah (v. 2) are that rock and quarry. A quarry at first contains only one column of rock; but from it many individual rocks are cut. The point is that the exiles had become so few, and were wondering how could they ever really be blessed again as God's people. To counter such thinking God reminds them, "Abraham was only one man, yet I blessed him, and multiplied him, just as I promised. Likewise, I will keep My promise to you" (vv. 2–3). Thus, though the exiles seem small in their own sight, they will soon be transformed into a great nation. And it is no mere coincidence that these words are intended to reach the ears of the exiles in the very land where Abraham first received his call. They are to imitate forefather Abraham, a model of righteousness through faith, coupled with obedience. We read that Abraham "believed in the Lord, and He reckoned it to him as righteousness" (Gen 15:6). And, that "by faith Abraham, when he was called, obeyed by going out . . . not knowing where he was going" (Heb 11:8).

But an appeal to the past is often so that one may see the future more clearly. "As I have done in the past, so I will do in the future," declares the Lord. Just as once the land of Israel was fruitful and beautiful—before the devastating armies of Babylon overran the countryside and towns, pillaging and burning—those desert like lands the Lord will again "make like Eden . . . the garden of the Lord" (v. 3). Again the streets of Zion (Jerusalem) will ring with songs of "joy and gladness," a theme already introduced in Isaiah 35:11. "Joy and gladness" often occur together in the Old Testament. Note, for example, Psalm 45:15 (in the context of a royal wedding), Psalm 51:8 (in the context of restoration from sin), and Zechariah 8:19 (in the context of the restoration of Jerusalem). The response of God's people to such a transformation will be "thanksgiving" (v. 3). Later, the prophet Jeremiah echoes the words of Isaiah when predicting the coming restoration of the exiles to Zion and the rebuilding of Zion itself:

> And from them shall proceed thanksgiving
> And the voice of those who make merry (Jer 30:19).

While the first stanza speaks of what God will do for His people in restoring Zion and Judah as an inhabitable place, *the view of the second stanza (vv. 4–6)* is worldwide and eschatological. God's "law" and "justice" will become "a light to the peoples" (v. 4), that is, the ethical and social benefits and demands of God's saving work will be available to all peoples. But God's justice also requires judgment, a judgment of "the peoples" (v. 5), but extending to all creation, in which the universe, subject to change and decay, will "vanish like smoke," followed by everlasting salvation and righteousness (v. 6). In this, then, there is also a promise of hope for creation (as there was for Zion in v. 3). Thus, verse 6 is a prologue to the announcement of the new heavens and new earth, although Isaiah delays this until Isa 65:17, where the promise of a newly created heavens and earth are the guarantee to God's servants of a newly created Jerusalem:

> For behold, I create new heavens and a new earth;

And the former things shall not be remembered or come to
  mind.
But be glad and rejoice forever in what I create;
For Behold I create Jerusalem for rejoicing,
And her people for gladness (Isa 65:17–18)

And again in Isaiah 66:22 where the permanence of the new
heavens and new earth is the guarantee of the permanence of
the continuing generations of God's people:

"For just as the new heavens and the new earth,
Which I make will endure before Me," declares the Lord,
"So your offspring and your name will endure."

The third stanza (vv. 7–8) is addressed to those among the
exiles who have found what they were looking for in verse 1, "in
whose heart is [God's] law" (v. 7). Thus, this stanza is addressed
to individual believers who are truly and ethically the people of
God, yet a people presently having to endure persecution by
their Babylonian captors. To such a persecuted people comes
the encouragement not to fear their enemies' "reproach" and
"reviling" (v. 7), for as is shown by the later prophet Zephaniah
(2:8–9), the enemies of God's people are the enemies of God,
with particular reference to the "reproach of Moab and the
reviling of Ammon." Such tyrants, says Isaiah, wear out like a
moth-eaten garment (v. 8; see also Isa 50:9), but God's
righteousness and salvation will never end (v. 8).

The lesson to be learned from this passage of Isaiah, and to
be lived by, is that the salvation of God is the only reality on
which God's people may rely in a universe that has been
destined to perish from the day of its creation. In the New
Testament, Peter urges God's people to allow this knowledge to
shape the way we live. "What sort of people ought you to be in
holy conduct and godliness?" Peter asks. "Since you look for
these things, be diligent to be found by Him in peace, spotless

and blameless . . . growing in the grace and knowledge of our Lord and Savior Jesus Christ." For only those who live righteously—walking with God by faith and in obedience, as did Enoch, Noah, Abraham, and a host of others who have come before—will find a place in the new heavens and new earth, for that is a place where only "righteousness dwells" (see 2 Pet 3:7–18 and Heb 11).

51:9–11. History and Eschatology

"Awake, awake" does not imply that Isaiah believes the Lord to be asleep and needs to be awakened, for he would surely agree with the Psalmist who declares that "He who guards Israel neither slumbers nor sleeps" (Ps 121:4). Rather it is a call to alert warriors that it is time to prepare for battle. Isaiah directs his call to the "arm of the Lord," one of his favorite metaphors for the Lord's power to save, (see also Isa 40:10; 51:5; 52:10; 53:1; 59:16; 62:8; 63:5, 12), and urges Him to "put on strength" (v. 9). "Put on" is used of a warrior putting on his armor (see 1 Sam 17:5, 38; Isa 59:17; Jer 46:4). Thus the opening of verse 9 is a call to the Lord, the Mighty Warrior, to battle.

This awakening is to be "as in the days of old" when the Lord "cut Rahab in pieces" (v. 9) When was this? When He "dried up the sea," and "made the depths of the sea a pathway"—a pathway "for the redeemed to cross over" (v. 10). This was the great salvation event of the Exodus of God's people out of Egypt, wrought in the crossing of the Red Sea. The Exodus event is what is meant when "Rahab" is mentioned. The name Rahab means the "boisterous one" or the "arrogant one." It is a name used several times for Egypt (see Isa 30:7; Psa 87:4). Also Egypt is referred to as the "sea

monster" (see Isa 27:1; Ezek 29:3; 32:2). When the Lord
demanded that the Pharaoh of Egypt let His people go free,
boisterous and arrogant Egypt defiantly refused. Then the arm
of the Lord swung into action, hewing into pieces and piercing
through the metaphorical "dragon" (v. 9). Thus the Lord
overcame Egypt. This metaphorical slaughter of the wild beast
is historical proof of the power of God. The mighty arm of the
Lord did such a mighty work once. Surely He can do it again.

This time the metaphorical "Rahab" will be Babylon. The
Lord's arm will overcome the defiance of Babylon. His
people—"the ransomed" (v. 11)—will be led out in a new
Exodus from Babylon "to Zion." The journey will be long, but
their entry into Zion will be accompanied by "joyful shouting."
A joy that cannot be quenched will take possession of the
returnees. But ultimately it is all the people of God, redeemed,
who will return to "everlasting joy," such a joy that "sorrow and
sighing will flee away" (see also Isa 25:8; 60:20; 65:19; Rev 7:17;
21:1, 4; 22:3). This eschatological hope of future redemption is
thus based on the solid foundation of God's power in historical
redemption.

51:12–16. The Lord's Reassuring Answer

The Lord's response to Isaiah's call for redemption is deeply
tender. The doubly emphatic "I" is intended to draw the Exile's
attention away from the momentary threat of their
oppressor—mighty Babylon—and to focus it upon Him and the
"comfort" He is offering (v. 12). As in Isaiah 40:1–2 and 51:3
comfort is much more than to merely give consolation to one *in*
his troubles; it is rather to deliver one *out* of his troubles.

The Exiles are fearful. God's word of comfort demands that
they examine the cause of their fear, the Babylonians, who are

138

mere human beings, "made like grass," destined to die (v. 12; a link with Isa 40:6–8). For their fear of their "oppressor," mere men, has caused them to forget "the Lord [their] Maker" (v. 13). In spite of their lack of faith—for this is indeed the basic cause of their fear—the Exiles are promised deliverance from bondage, death and hunger (v. 14). This promise is made on the authority of the Creator who stretched out the heavens and laid the foundations of the earth (v. 16). It is only when we ignore such mighty and enduring works of God that we can fall into fear of mere men who oppose God.

51:17–23. The Cup of God's Anger

Isaiah now turns to Jerusalem with a call similar to that in verse 9, "Awaken yourself! Awaken yourself!" (v. 17). This time, however, Jerusalem, is indeed asleep, a sleep of "devastation and destruction" (v. 19). The appeal is to awaken herself in anticipation of her day of deliverance. With her inhabitants in bondage in Babylon, Jerusalem is also metaphorically in bondage. So when God delivers the Exiles, Jerusalem too will know deliverance.

Isaiah follows his appeal with a most descriptive picture of the desolation and suffering of Jerusalem. Jerusalem's suffering is not attributed to the mere chances of history, but to "the Lord's hand." The city is graphically pictured as a woman staggering about in a drunken stupor. She holds in her hand an empty cup, called "the cup of His anger" and "the chalice of reeling." It is empty because she has "drained it to the dregs" (v. 17). The tragedy of it all is that even natural familial help and sympathy are missing. Where normally one of her "sons" would step forward to steady her, perhaps even carry her home in arms of love, no son steps forward to do so (v. 18). Why?

139

Because they too are drunk with the wrath of the Lord, and are passed out and lie in the streets, helpless "like a [wild] antelope [caught] in a net" (v. 20).

The remainder of this passage, however, depicts one of God's great reversals of history. God has taken "the cup of reeling" and "the chalice of [His] anger" from the hand of the exiled inhabitants of Jerusalem, and has put it now into the hand of those who torment them—their Babylonian oppressors (v. 22). The Lord is indignant over the extreme cruelties practiced against the defeated people of God. The usual symbolic gesture of conquest is seen in Joshua's command to his military chiefs when he defeated five enemy kings: "put your feet on the necks of these kings" (Josh 10:24. See also Ps 110:1, "enemies a footstool for Your feet"). Babylon had gone far beyond this and had even made them "lie down" in rows so that their backs were like the paved surface of a street "for those who walk over it" (v. 23). Here is a link with Isaiah's earlier expression of the Lord's indignation at haughty Babylon's degradation of His people: "I . . . gave them into your hand, [but] you did not show mercy to them" (Isa 47:6).

Thus, those who take unfair advantage of the weak, those who practice cruelty will suffer cruelty in return—at the hand of the Lord!

YOUR GOD REIGNS! (ISAIAH 52)

This section has three major units:

- ❑ Zion, Awake! (vv. 1–6).
- ❑ Good News of Redemption (vv. 7–10).
- ❑ Depart from Babylon! (vv. 11–12).
- ❑ God Reports on His Servant (vv. 13–15).

52:1–6. Zion, Awake!

The idea here is that Zion, which has lain in dust and chains throughout these many years of her people's captivity, is to put on her best festal clothes for a celebration of the end of the exile.

Verses (52:)1–2 contain a series of commands addressed to Zion that are in direct contrast to those commands spoken to Babylon in the taunt-song of Isaiah 47:1–2. In the former, Babylon the Queen is reduced to the status of slave; in the latter, Zion is raised from the status of slave to that of Queen. Note the contrasts as given in *Table 2: Contrast between Babylon and Zion* on page 168.

Thus Isaiah foresees a time when the roles of the two cities will be completely reversed: Babylon will be abased while Zion will be exalted.

Verses (52:) 3–6 point to the link between the first exodus from Egypt and this new exodus from Babylon. It is in the context of this historic link that the Lord justifies His present deliverance of His people from Babylon: "You were sold for nothing" (v. 3). Babylon had acquired God's people but had paid nothing for them. Therefore God's people can be "redeemed without money" (v. 3), simply on the strength of a divine order.

Isaiah suggests that a historic pattern has prevailed during the entirety of Israel's existence (v. 4). At the beginning of her existence, Israel had gone down into Egypt as a guest. Egypt had no rightful claim on her, but when Moses demanded her release, Pharaoh violated her rights. Centuries later Assyria appeared on the scene of history. Though God used Assyria as a tool in His hands to punish Israel (see Isa 10:5–6), as a nation Assyria, who had no rightful claims on Israel, "oppressed them without cause" (v. 4).

The Lord's question, "Now therefore, what do I have here?" (v. 5) concerns the present situation of His people's captivity in the context of the historic pattern: again His people had "been taken away without cause" (v. 5), that is, Babylon has no rightful claim upon Israel. Yet she had treated captive Israel with oppression as though she had due right and title to what she held, all the time "howling," or "shrieking out" words of blasphemy against the name of the Lord (v. 5). These blasphemous words were perhaps as the Psalmist records the nations saying: "Where now is their God?" (Ps 115:2).

All this justifies the Lord's deliverance of His people from captivity. And in this deliverance God's people will come to a more true and deeper knowledge of the Lord. "My people shall know my name," says the Lord (v. 6). To know God's name is to experience the saving effects of His redemption power, and to enter into an intimate relationship of fellowship with Him. The discouraged, despairing people of Zion were to experience this as God would again stand in their midst and declare, "Here I am" (v. 6).

And this heart transforming, spirit uplifting, sudden presence of God in the midst of His discouraged and despairing followers would be repeated again and again. Witness the experience of the two discouraged New Testament disciples on the road to Emmaus when Jesus came suddenly to walk with them: "Were not our hearts burning within us?"(Luke 24:13–35). Witness the larger group of disciples gathered that same night in Jerusalem when Jesus suddenly appeared in their midst, and their troubled and doubting hearts were filled with joy (Luke 24:36–43). My friends, the present is no different than the past. The Lord still suddenly makes His Presence known to you and me in those times when our spiritual eyes are veiled because of some seemingly hopeless circumstance over which we have no control. In those times He comes and says "Here I am" and our spirit is uplifted and our discouragement vanishes.

52:7–10. Good News of Redemption

Here is a beautiful poem built around the themes of redemption, the reign of God and universal salvation. Each verse adds a new thought to the whole.

First we see a solitary runner crossing the mountains between Babylon and Jerusalem, bringing the good news of well-being ("peace") and deliverance, and that God is truly King (v. 7). *Then* the watchmen on the walls of Jerusalem see the runner and, beyond him, God Himself bringing the exiles back to Jerusalem (a link with Isa 40:9–11). They break into a unison song of rejoicing (v. 8). *Finally*, the ruins of Jerusalem themselves join in the rejoicing at the prospect of comfort and redemption (v. 9).

The purpose of all this is not just the good of Israel, but the ultimate spread of the knowledge of God's salvation to the very ends of the earth (v. 10).

52:11–12. Depart from Babylon!

There are clear echoes of the first exodus here, but the big difference is that this time they will not have to hurry (v. 12) as they did out of Egypt (Exod 12:11, 33). They will journey across the distance between Babylon and Jerusalem in peace and security, without anxiety. For just as the Ark of the Covenant had gone before the Israelites and the pillar of cloud had protected their rear in the first exodus, so God will now go before them and behind them to be their rear guard.

52:13—53:12. The Fourth Servant Song: The Servant's Victory[1]

This Servant Song opens with the words, "Behold, My Servant." These are the identical words with which the first Servant Song opens (Isa 42:1–4), thus linking the two Songs. The first indicates the origin of the Servant, the last the culmination of His work.

This fourth Servant Song is most often given a title that highlights the suffering of the Servant. Isaiah's primary concern, however, is not with the Servant's suffering, but with His triumph over suffering. Therefore, all references to His suffering are to be translated in the past tense. For example: "He *was*

---

[1] For the other three Servant Songs see the comments on Isaiah 42:1–4; 49:1–6; 50:4–9.

despised and forsaken" (Isa 53:3); "He *was* wounded for our transgressions" (Isa 53:5); "He *was* cut off out of the land of the living" (Isa 53:8). All references to His triumph and glory, however, are to be translated in the future tense. For example: "My Servant *will* prosper" (Isa 52:13); "He *will* see His offspring, He *will* prolong His days" (Isa 53:10); "He *will* divide the booty with the strong" (Isa 53:12).

This Servant Song greatly influenced the New Testament writers' understanding of the gospel and the problem of the crucified Messiah. Of the twelve verses in Isaiah 53, only one is not quoted in whole or in part in the New Testament. These quotations are found in all four Gospels, in Acts, Romans, Philippians, Hebrews and 1 Peter.

52:13–15. God Reports on His Servant

These three verses contain in summary form what is unfolded more fully in chapter 53 but with the thought in reverse order. Here, exaltation is stressed first, then humiliation; in chapter 53, humiliation comes first, followed by exaltation.

God announces that His Servant will be exalted (v. 13). The Servant will achieve what He sets out to do. This is the fundamental theme, the theme with which the Song also closes (Isa 53:11–12). Everything else in the Song must be viewed in the light of this ultimate exaltation of the Servant.

Verse 14 is a sudden and shocking contrast. The Servant will suffer terrible humiliation, almost beyond human belief. He has become so disfigured through suffering that He hardly appears human, causing astonishment in those who see Him. This picture is expanded in Isaiah 53:2–9.

145

The verb of the first line of verse 15 occurs only here in the Old Testament, and its meaning is unclear. It could be either "Thus He will *sprinkle* many nations" or "Thus He will *startle* many nations." "Startle" fits better with the implication of the rest of the verse, that the suffering of the Servant is a matter of surprise, horror and disbelief to others. Thus, the nations will be startled when they see the Servant's sudden rise from humiliation to exaltation.

WE ARE HEALED BY HIS STRIPES
(ISAIAH 53)

This chapter can be divided into two units:
- ❏ Others Report on the Servant (vv. 1–11a).
- ❏ God's Final Verdict on His Servant (vv. 11b–12).

53:1–11a. Others Report on the Servant

Unnamed speakers begin to give their report, but they question if anyone will believe it since it is so amazing. The report concerning this Servant is so unprecedented and unexpected, indeed, so unique, that it seems unbelievable.

Who are these speakers, the "We" of the Song? Some suggest that they are the "many nations" of Isaiah 52:15, others that it is the Israelites witnessing what happens to the Servant in their midst, or Isaiah speaking as "we" on their behalf. Perhaps if we bring the New Testament to bear upon this passage, we can overhear believers discussing the tragic death of the Servant of the Lord. Luke's account would be a good parallel (Isa 24:13-35). Here we see and hear two disciples on the Emmaus road, discussing the recent events of the death of Christ, then later that same night, reporting to the others that He had indeed appeared to them. At first they had completely misunderstood His death, but now they have a totally new understand with Christ-opened eyes.

We must see verses 2–9 as covering a whole lifespan of suffering, from "He grew up" (v. 2) through until "His grave was assigned" (v. 9). ***Verses 2–3*** speak specifically of the Servant's suffering and rejection. He was one without visible evidence of God's blessing, and therefore without respect from his fellowmen (v. 2). In fact, He was "forsaken of men," literally "ceasing from the company of men" (v. 3). Why? Jewish theology in both Old Testament times and in Jesus' day assumed that such suffering must be the punishment of God for sins. Thus, 'we' despised the Servant because it seemed obvious to them that He stood under some terrible judgment of God—for His *own* sins!

Verses 4–6 speak of the Servant's vicarious suffering, that is, in the place of and for the sake of someone else. In a sudden and shocking reversal of opinion, the "we" now confess that they had been entirely wrong about the Servant. It is true that His suffering was a punishment from God, but not for His own sins. Rather, all the suffering that He bore had been for *their* "transgressions and iniquities" (v. 5). They do not say how this change of mind ("conversion") has taken place, or how the exchange of penalties takes place. All they do is reflect on the contrast between who the Servant is and what He suffered, and who they are and how they deserved to suffer. This reflection moves them to repentance and to find in the Servant their own "well-being" (lit., peace) and "healing."

There could be no clearer expression of vicarious suffering. The Hebrew word order is significant, placing great emphasis upon the "our" and "He." "Surely it was *our* griefs *He* was bearing, and it was *our* pains *He* was carrying" (v. 5). The paradox is that the One who did not deserve to suffer at all was the One who had suffered the most—for us!

Verse 6 begins and ends with the same Hebrew word meaning "all of us." It also contains a threefold description of sin: it is universal ("all we"), it separates and scatters ("have gone astray"), and it is essentially self-willed ("to his own way").

In verses 7–9 the anonymous speakers speak of the Servant's death, a death resulting from a legal trial in which the Servant suffers what His judges believe to be right—because He does not defend himself.

In His trial He was "oppressed and afflicted" (v. 7), that is, harshly treated. The New Testament writers tell us that Jesus, in His trial before Pilate, was whipped, and a crown of thorns put upon his head. Some spat upon Him, while others hit Him in the face and on the head (John 19:1–3; Matt 27:28–30). The speakers liken the Servant to a sheep (v. 7). In this they point out a deliberate contrast between "all of us" who *like sheep* have gone astray, and the Servant who *like a sheep* has been sacrificed for us all.

The Servant did not receive a fair trial, they say (v. 8). "By oppression and judgment," that is, after arrest and without proper judgment "He was taken away." Moreover, nobody among His contemporaries—"as for His generation"—imagined that His being "cut off", a sudden and violent death, was actually for their "transgression."

Even in His burial, proper norms were not followed. It was usual to be buried in the same tomb with the bones of members of one's family. To be denied that was a great shame and disgrace. Rather, the Servant is identified with "wicked men" even in His death. His grave is to be where criminals are buried (v. 9). The Hebrew parallelism of this verse, "with wicked men" // "with a rich man", suggests that the wicked are to be equated with the rich, as the Old Testament so often does (see Prov 11:16; Jer 17:11; Mic 6:12).

149

The speakers, however, now speak again (cf. v. 5) from the viewpoint of their subsequent conversion. They now realize the truth: the Servant Himself had not deserved what He suffered at all:

> He had done no violence,
> Nor was there any deceit in His mouth (v. 9).

The verdict and execution were all wrong! Thus verse 9 ends with a ringing affirmation of the Servant's innocence.

In verses 10–11a the speakers discuss the Servant's resurrection. It is clear that they envision an ongoing work of the Servant *after* His sufferings and death; they portray His ministry as coming to a climax beyond the grave.

The first two lines of verse 10 are a clear statement that the death of the Servant, though it was a complete denial of justice, was no accident of history. It was in fact the plan and will of God himself. To say that "the Lord was pleased to crush" the Servant means that the events leading up to his death were part of God's plan to overcome sin. The Lord permitted Him to suffer, not out of anger toward Him, but out of His deep love toward sinners. The apostle John tells us that "God so loved the world, that He gave His only begotten Son, that whoever believes in Him should not perish, but have eternal life" (John 3:16).

The latter part of verse 10 indicates that once the Servant has offered Himself as a "guilt offering," certain results will follow. The Servant will see His "offspring" and "prolong His days." The offspring should be understood not as His physical but as His spiritual descendants. Through *them* the work that God has entrusted to His care, the work of salvation, will be carried on—will "prosper in His hand."

53:11b–12. God's Final Verdict on His Servant

This Servant Song now reverts to first person speech by God, who gives His verdict. "The Righteous one, My Servant" was in the right all the time. He is the "Righteous One" who by His own experience ("knowledge" in verse 11 implies a knowledge gained through experience), will "make the many righteous." Those who are wicked will come to be accounted righteous through *Him*. The mission of the Servant is inseparably linked with righteousness and justice, here in the sense of our personal salvation.

Verse 12 celebrates the Servant's exaltation in the traditional language of victory: the distribution of the spoils of war after the battle has been won. He will be exalted because He was willing to be abased, and to be "numbered with the transgressors."

This fourth Servant Song comes to a climax on the note of the Servant's continuing intercessory ministry on behalf of the very "transgressors" among whom He was numbered. What does it mean to "intercede" on behalf of a transgressor? The Hebrew term used here means to interpose or to intervene. Thus, to intercede is much more than merely to pray for one who has transgressed. It is to put oneself in the place of transgressors, and thus to take upon oneself the full impact of the punishment due them. To intercede, then, means to intervene between a man and the consequences of his sin. This is precisely what Jesus did when He offered Himself upon the cross in our behalf. Peter says, "He Himself bore our sins in His body on the cross, that we might die to sin and live to righteousness; for by His wounds [we are] healed" (1 Pet 2:24; see also Heb 9:28).

151

Isaiah 53

True intercession is always more than prayer. It involves a way of life, for we cannot offer intercessory prayer unless we are living intercessory lives. How can I pray to God on behalf of the needy unless I am willing to involve myself in their situation, to share in their griefs, to bear their hurts? This question I address equally to myself as I do to you.

FEAR NOT! THE LORD HAS CALLED YOU (ISAIAH 54)

This chapter has four major units:

- ❑ The Enlargement of Jerusalem (vv. 1–3).
- ❑ Jerusalem's Reconciliation to God (vv. 4–8).
- ❑ A Covenant of Peace (vv. 9–10).
- ❑ Jerusalem, Beautiful and Invincible (vv. 11–17).

54:1–3. The Enlargement of Jerusalem

Isaiah's vivid description of the desolate city here picks up his earlier imagery in Isaiah 49:4–23, that is, Jerusalem as an abandoned, barren wife (compare Jeremiah's imagery in Lam 1:1–2). But there is promise here: the Lord intends to take her back, and she will soon become the mother of many children (v. 1). In fact, her children will be so numerous that there will be no room in the present city to house them. Thus she is told to build a larger "tent" in which to house her family. And the larger the tent, the longer the ropes and the stronger the stakes must be (v. 2).[1] The promise goes farther: Jerusalem's

---

[1] Isaiah 54:2 was the text from which William Carey, on May 31, 1792, preached before a group of Baptist ministers in Kettering, England. His sermon had two points: (1) expect great things from God, and (2) attempt great things for God. This sermon generated great response, leading to the

population will overflow her walls and spread "to the right and to the left", taking possession of nations and inhabiting their cities (v. 3).

54:4–8. Jerusalem's Reconciliation to God

In imagery similar to that of Hosea, Isaiah depicts the restoration of Israel to God's favor (see Hos 2:14–20). The shame of her youth (perhaps referring to Israel's ancient Egyptian bondage) and the reproach of her "widowhood" (surely referring to her more recent exile in Babylon) will be remembered no more (v. 4). Rather, she will be reconciled to her "husband," who is none other than her "Maker" and "Redeemer," "the Lord of Hosts," "the Holy One of Israel," even "the God of all the earth" (v. 5).

God's "anger" is but for a moment in the face of His "great compassion" and "everlasting lovingkindness" (vv. 7–8). Here are two of the most important ideas of the Old Testament. *Compassion* speaks of God's pity for humankind in their frailty, misery and weakness. David wrote:

> Just as a father has compassion on his children,
> So the Lord has compassion on those who fear Him.
> For He Himself knows our frame;
> He is mindful that we are but dust (Ps 103:13–14).

Everlasting lovingkindness carries the idea of loyalty or reliability. It is a covenant term. Thus, Israel can be assured of the utter loyalty of the One who makes the covenant. God's compassion, which has moved Him to take Israel unto Himself

---

formation of the Baptist Missionary Society, opening the door for the modern missionary movement.

again, is rooted in His very character. He and His covenant are utterly reliable.

54:9–10. A Covenant of Peace.

In a departure from his previous use of the Exodus as a comparative backdrop for what God is now doing, Isaiah depicts the period of Israel's exile in Babylon as like the days of the flood in Noah's time (v. 9). After the flood, God made a covenant with Noah, a covenant that guaranteed the survival of the world and the human race (see Gen 9:8–17). Its counterpart here is a "covenant of peace" (v. 10), a covenant more durable and unbreakable than the covenant with Noah. One may see mountains removed and hills shaken, but the covenant of peace will never be withdrawn (v. 10). Here, Isaiah is in tune with the Psalmist, who said:

> God is our refuge and strength,
> A very present help in trouble
> Therefore we will not fear, though the earth should change,
> And though the mountains slip into the heart of the sea;
> Though its waters roar and foam,
> Though the mountains quake at its swelling pride (Ps 46:1–3).

54:11–17. Jerusalem, Beautiful and Invincible.

In verses (54:) 11–12 Isaiah gives a picture that is both literal and figurative. It is partly literal in that it envisions the rebuilding of Jerusalem itself after the Jews' return from exile. But it is also figurative of the "city of God" as depicted in Revelation 21:9–21, with its use of all kinds of precious stones as building material for its oundations, walls and gates. The future city of God will be one of rare beauty and splendor, indeed, a city redeemed and recreated by the God of all the earth. Jerusalem, then, becomes a type of the new creation.

Verses (54:)13–17 depict an idyllic situation in which Jerusalem's inhabitants are blessed with prosperity and freedom from oppression and terror. Verse 13 gives some of the spiritual values of the redeemed Jerusalem. "All your sons shall be taught by the Lord." God-inspired knowledge will be given to the children of God. To possess such knowledge will mean to possess eternal life (see John 6:45–47). Verse 14 gives the foundation for such prosperity and freedom: *righteousness.* Jerusalem's future establishment as a city of righteousness is a theme found throughout the whole book of Isaiah:

> Then I will restore your judges as at the first, and your
> counselors as at the beginning;
> After that you will be called the city of *righteousness*, a faithful
> city (Isa 1:26).

> Behold, I am laying in Zion a stone, a tested stone,
> A costly cornerstone for the foundation, firmly placed.
> He who believes in it will not be disturbed.
> And I will make justice the measuring line,
> And *righteousness* the level (Isa 28:16–17).

> The Lord is exalted, for He dwells on high;
> He has filled Zion with justice and *righteousness* (Isa 33:5).

> And I will make peace your administrators,
> And *righteousness* your overseers (Isa 60:17)

> Then all your people will be *righteous*;
> They will possess the land forever (Isa 60:21).

This foundation of righteousness leads to the final promise of verse 17: God will publicly vindicate Israel and protect her from the weapons and accusing tongues of her enemies. Does Israel merit such mercy? Indeed not. Isaiah is evangelical here. God's grace is free. He gives unmerited pardon!

O THIRSTY, COME TO THE WATERS!
(ISAIAH 55)

This chapter has four major units:

- ❑ God's Generosity (vv. 1–5).
- ❑ Called to Repentance (vv. 6–9).
- ❑ God's Word Never Fails (vv. 10–11).
- ❑ The New Exodus (vv. 12–13).

This chapter concludes the section of Isaiah's prophecy addressed primarily to the Jews in Babylonian exile (chapters 40–55). We have given the title *Our Incomparable God* to this entire section, for this is what Isaiah has been trying to get the exiled Jews to see: that there is simply no other so-called god—in Babylon or elsewhere—with whom the Living God can be compared. And it is this incomparable God who now extends a gracious, but urgent, invitation to get in line with what God is now doing. Don't delay! Join the victory march! Be one of those who are willing to leave the relatively comfortable but spiritually unsatisfying life of exile in Babylon. For what? For a great redemption that includes: spiritual nourishment (vv. 1–2), a renewal of the covenant (vv. 3–5), mercy and pardon (vv. 6–7), and an unsurpassed joy (vv. 12–13).

55:1–5. God's Generosity

The assumption here is that all people "thirst," both physically and spiritually. And what better can quench thirst than "water"? Yes, water, and even "wine and milk" are offered without charge to any who is thirsty. Water, wine and milk are symbols of the redemption that God is offering: freedom from the slavery of exile. But to avail oneself of this redemption, one must "come" to where the water, wine and milk are (v. 1). And these will not be found in Babylon, where to remain will continue to require one to spend money "for what does not satisfy" (v. 2). The things of Babylon, the place of exile, are not the real "bread" of life. Here we hear echoes of the age-old truth, spoken by Moses to the Israelites at the end of their Exodus journey, just before they crossed into the land of Canaan: "A person does not live by bread alone" (Deut 8:3). By what, then does one live? What is real bread? God, Himself, is. In another time long after the period of exile, perhaps with the words of both Moses and Isaiah in mind, Jesus said to some later-day Israelites, "I am the bread of life; the one who comes to Me shall not hunger, and the one who believes in Me shall never thirst" (John 6:35).

The language of Isaiah speaks of an "abundance" (v. 2), free, all at God's expense! The invitation is "come to Me", and in coming you will find "life," real life (v. 3). Again, one is reminded of Jesus' words: *"I came that they might have life, and might have [it] abundantly"* (John 10:10).

How sure is this promise of salvation and abundance? Just as sure as were the covenant promises made to King David in the past (v. 3). God had promised to David, who in his younger days was only a shepherd, a royal dynasty and a kingdom. God had fulfilled His promise to David; a knowledge of the past would confirm this. Just so, He would now fulfill *this* promise to His people in exile. Moreover, God had made David "a witness to the peoples" (v. 4) of the greatness of Israel's God. Just so, God will now place this responsibility of witnessing upon His

159

people brought out of exile. Their commission now is to make known to the nations the "Holy One of Israel" (v. 5). Here is a far-reaching prediction that extends into New Testament times, and even onward to us today. Paul wrote, *"For they are not all Israel who are [descended] from Israel"* (Rom 9:6). By this he means that the Israel of the Old Testament, with the coming of the New Testament, becomes the "Israel of God" (Gal 6:16). And *this* Israel is made up of those who have *"become children of God"* through belief in Jesus (John 1:12). And whenever and wherever the gospel is witnessed to the nations of this world, there is fulfillment of this passage.

55:6–9. Called to Repentance

God is not always accessible, it seems. Sometimes He must withdraw His presence. So the time to "seek the Lord" through prayer and repentance is "while He is near" (v. 6). This call to repentance is both general and specific. It certainly applies to mankind everywhere and at all times. But in the specific context of the Exile, the call is to those who confuse their own thoughts and ways with those of God (v. 8–9). "We don't understand nor approve of what God is doing," they say. "His ways are beyond our finite comprehension. After all, wasn't it God, Himself, who commanded us to build homes, to plant gardens, to take wives for our sons and give our daughters to husbands that they might give us grandchildren, so that we might multiply here? (see Jer 29:5–6). It seems best to us to remain here in Babylon. Here we know what we have. Why set out into the unknown, heading for a place filled with unknowns? No, we will do nothing."

Such thoughts are "wicked" and "unrighteous," says Isaiah (v. 7). The call now is to "forsake," make a complete break with the ways of Babylon into which many have become to deeply immersed. This is the negative side of repentance. The positive side is to "return to the Lord" with whom there is great "compassion" and "abundant pardon" (v. 7). Thus, the essence of repentance is a turning away from and a turning unto. In the New Testament, Paul, in commending the Christians at Thessalonica, reverses the order: *"you turned to God from idols"* (1 Thess 1:9).

55:10–11. God's Word Never Fails

Now, at the close of this section of his prophecy, a prophecy to the exiles in Babylon, Isaiah repeats the note on which he began: the enduring, mighty power of *"the word of our God [which] stands forever"* (Isa 40:6–8). Here is a final reassurance to the exiles that everything that he, Isaiah the prophet, has said concerning God's plan for them, will come to fulfillment. Just as surely as new growth comes to fields that have been watered by the "rain and the snow . . . from heaven," so will the city of Jerusalem be restored and re-inhabited, and individuals' hearts will be morally and spiritually regenerated: if they will but receive and act upon God's word.

55:12–13. The New Exodus

The exiles' departure from Babylon is pictured as a victory march, a new victorious exodus of the people of God. They "go out with joy" for God leads them "forth in peace" (v. 12). So Isaiah comes back again to another of his introductory notes: Jerusalem's and the exiles' "warfare is ended" (Isa 40:2). But "peace" (Heb. *shalom*) in the Old Testament is more than merely the absence or cessation of war. It is *wholeness,* a wholeness that includes forgiveness, pardon and restoration. And the wholeness extends even to the transformation and rejoicing of nature. We hear the mountains and hills singing; we see trees clapping their hands, our eyes feast upon deserts transformed into memorial gardens—all as an everlasting tribute to the redemptive power of our God, the Holy One of Israel. Here, Isaiah is eschatological. The exiles' redemption from Babylon and triumphant march to Jerusalem, and the subsequent restoration of Jerusalem itself, is but a foreshadow of the final glorious *"new Jerusalem coming down out of heaven from God"* (Rev 21:2), into which God will bring His bride, *"those whose names are written in the Lamb's book of life"* (Rev 21:27). There, in that New Jerusalem, weeping, mourning and pain, even death itself, will find no place, for all these belong to the old Jerusalem. In their place will be *"the spring of the water of life without cost"* (Rev 21:6), *"a well of water springing up to eternal life"* (John 4:14).

CONCLUSION

The central theme of Isaiah's message in chapters 40–55 is *salvation*. Thus, it is proper to speak of the "gospel" of Isaiah. Though the prophet addresses the people of God as a whole, the word of God that has come to him to proclaim is intended personally for each individual. Beginning with God's ringing call, "Comfort, comfort my people" (Isa 40:1), to the closing exultation, "You will go out with joy" (Isa 55:12), salvation is exultantly proclaimed, promised, and witnessed to throughout this "gospel." This note of exultation that rings throughout the prophet's preaching is highlighted by the use of language in praise of God.

There is praise for God's divine majesty (Isa 40:12–31). This praise intends to enable the Jewish exiles to recapture their (earlier) vision of God as powerful enough to miraculously deliver them from Babylonian exile. And if he can deliver them, he can carry them safely on the long and dangerous journey back home to their beloved Jerusalem.

There is praise for God as Redeemer (Isa 44:24a), who is then extolled as Creator (Isa 44:24b) and lord of history (Isa 44:25).

There is praise for the consistency between what God says and what he does. This is highlighted in the several trial scenes (Isa 41:1–5, 21–29; 43:8–15; 44:6–8; 45:20–25), in which the Lord and the gods of the nations confront one another, where the question to be answered is, who is truly God? Is there continuity in the Lord's advance announcement of an event—here the doom and exile of Israel—and it actual realization? In this, insists Isaiah, God proved himself to be God: he both announced the forthcoming doom and then made it happen. Therefore, since the Lord has proved himself trustworthy in the past, Israel may confidently place their trust in his present word of coming salvation.

There is praise for the Lord's uniqueness: "I am the first and I am the last, / And there is no God besides Me" (Isa 44:6; see also 41:4; 44:8; 45:5, 6, 21; 46:4; 48:12). None of the gods of Babylon and the nations can make this claim. According to the ancient near eastern myths, each of the gods (Marduk, Bel, Nebo, etc.) had a created beginning, and each could be brought to an end through death. Israel's God makes the claim that he encompasses all of existence from start to finish. He is before time (which he has created) and will still be when time is no more (which he will abolish). The Psalmist (Ps 90:2) affirms this conviction when he says:

> Before the mountains were born,
> Or Thou didst give birth to the earth and the world,
> Even from everlasting to everlasting, Thou art God.

The title "first and last" is ascribed to Jesus Christ four times in the New Testament book of Revelation (Rev 1:17; 2:8; 21:6; 22:13), an indication that the early Church was convinced that Christ was indeed the incarnate creating and saving God of the Old Testament.

There are exultant songs of praise, indicating a response in faith that God is who he says he is and will do what he promises to do.

> Sing to the Lord a new song,
> *Sing* His praise from the end of the earth!
> You who go down to the sea, and all that is in it.
> You islands and those who dwell on them (Isa 42:10).

164

> Shout for joy, O heavens, for the LORD has done *it!*
> Shout joyfully, you lower parts of the earth;
> Break forth into a shout of joy, you mountains,
> O forest, and every tree in it;
> For the LORD has redeemed Jacob
> And in Israel He shows His glory (Isa 44:23).

> Shout for joy, O heavens! And rejoice, O earth!
> Break forth into joyful shouting, O mountains!
> For the LORD has comforted His people.
> And will have compassion on His afflicted (Isa 49:13).

> Break forth, shout joyfully together,
> You waste places of Jerusalem;
> For the Lord has comforted His people,
> He has redeemed Jerusalem.
> The LORD has bared His holy arm
> In the sight of all the nations;
> That all the ends of the earth may see
> The salvation of our God (Isa 52:9–10).

This latter exultant song of joy (Isa 52:9–10) is in acknowledgment of the one who brings "good news" of "peace" (lit., well-being, wholeness, Heb. *shalom*) and "happiness" (lit., good),

> Who announces salvation,
> *And* says to Zion, 'Your God reigns!' (Isa 52:7).

This is gospel!

God's salvation is highlighted in chapter 53. Here the Servant of the Lord, of whom Jesus Christ is the fulfillment, bears our "griefs" and "sorrows" (v. 4), the responsibility for our "iniquities" (vv. 5, 6), and our "sin" (v. 12) upon himself. He accepts in our place the ultimate punishment of self-sacrifice,

Conclusion

"Like a lamb that is led to slaughter" (v. 7), "Although He had done no violence" (v. 9).

There is the clarion call to every one who is spiritually thirsty" to "come to the waters" of salvation (Isa 55:1). Jeremiah will later speak of God as the "fountain of living waters" (Jer 2:13; 17:13). Jesus, even still later at the well of Jacob in Sychar, no doubt with this Old Testament imagery in the background, will offer to the Samaritan woman dying of spiritual thirst, the "living water" of salvation that would become within her "a well of water springing up to eternal life."

Thus, in this section of his prophecy (chapters 40-55), as indeed elsewhere throughout his book, Isaiah presents a full "gospel." Interpreted in the light of the New Testament, this gospel calls us to come to God, the Fountain of Living Water, to allow our sins and spiritual sicknesses to be lifted from us by his Servant, the eternal Son, Jesus Christ, and to accept the indwelling presence of the God's Holy Spirit.

My friend, when this transforming experience becomes your personal experience, as you go about your daily lives, in both the good and the bad times

> You will go out with joy,
> And be led forth with peace,

And it will truly seem that

> The mountains and the hills will break forth into shouts of joy before you,
> And all the trees of the field will clap *their* hands (Isa 55:12).

TABLES

Table 1: Isaiah's Prophecy and Its Fulfillment in NT[1]

The Prophecy	The Fulfillment
He will be exalted (Isa 52:13)	Phil 2:9
He will be disfigured by suffering (Isa 52:14; 53:2)	Mark 15:17, 19
He will make a blood atonement (Isa 52:15)	1 Pet 1:2
He will be widely rejected (Isa 53:1, 3)	John 12:37, 38
He will bear the sins and sorrows (Isa 53:4, 5)	Rom 4:25; 1 Pct 2:24, 25
He will be our substitute (Isa 53:6, 8)	2 Cor 5:21
He will voluntarily accept our guilt & punishment (Isa 53:7,8)	John 10:11; 19:30
He will be buried in a rich man's tomb (Isa 53:9)	John 19:38–42
He will save us who believe in Him (Isa 53:12	John 3:16; Acts 16:31
He will die on behalf of transgressors (Isa 53:12)	Mark 15:27, 28; Luke 22:37

---

[1] Adapted from *The Wesley Bible.* (Nashville: Thomas Nelson Publishers, 1990) p. 1059.

Tables

Table 2: Contrast between Babylon and Zion

Babylon (Isa 47:1–2)	Zion (Isa 52:1–2)
Come down and sit in the dust. Sit on the ground without a throne. Take the millstones and grind meal. Remove your veil, strip off the skirt. Uncover the leg.	Clothe yourself in . . . strength. Clothe yourself in . . . beautiful garments. Shake yourself from the dust. Rise up. Loose yourself from the chains.